The Way We Were

Oliver C. Harper

To my good friend Dean
Ofipr

PRESS

The Way We Were
by Oliver C. Harper

Printed in the United States of America

ISBN 9781613792032

www.xulonpress.com

I would like to thank my wife, Joan, for the many hours she spent editing the following pages. I would also like to thank my youngest son, Bob, for helping to prepare the book for publishing.

All pictures are from the author's own private collection unless otherwise noted.

Contents

PROLOGUE

The author and his family

R ev. Harper was born August 10, 1914 on a farm northeast of Sunset, Texas. In the Summer of 1932, Oliver left home to seek work and further his education in Wichita Falls. He almost joined the Navy but by a stroke of <u>fate</u> he was offered a job at Sears. There, he made $12.50 per week in the auto-service department. During this time, he met Marie Dollard, who, at that time, was the organist at the First Christian Church of Wichita Falls. They later married in 1938 and their union produced two sons, John C. and Robert L. Harper. He and Marie made a superb musical team with her accompanying his vocal talent on the piano or organ.

After World War II, Rev. Harper further utilize these talents by enrolling at Texas Christian University and Brite Divinity School. He was later ordained by the First Christian Church in Wichita Falls in 1951. Rev. Harper served churches in Moran, Dallas, Troy, Holland, Rogers, Quanah, Freeport, Vernon, and Fort Worth. While in Vernon, he and Marie hosted a radio devotional program every morning on KVWC for about 5 years. Rev. Harper was involved in a number of revivals throughout Texas. Also, while in Vernon, he served as a guidance counselor for the Christian Youth Fellowship Conference.

Rev. Harper was an endowed member of the Scottish Rite. While serving the Troy, Holland and Rogers churches, Rev. Harper was raised to the sublime degree of a Master Mason in Rogers Lodge 602 in 1954. He and Marie were both active in the Order Of The Eastern Star while in Vernon. And he later served as Grand Prelate of the Nights Templar in 1964. Finally, he was a recipient of the Golden Trowel Award in 2003 by Nocona Lodge 753.

After his retirement in 1976, he served as interim minister in Bowie, Brownwood, Graham Iowa Park and Nocona. He was awarded the title of Minister Emeritus in both Central Christian Church in Nocona and the First Christian Church in Vernon. In 1980, Oliver was recognized, by the Disciples of Christ brotherhood, as Small Congregation Minister Of The Year. His beloved wife of 60 years died in 1998. Fourteen years later Rev. Harper moved from Nocona to a retirement home in Wichita Falls. There, he met and married Joan Kelley in 2005. In 2008, he was declared Elder Emeritus by the First Christian Church in Wichita Falls. Overall, he served for 53 years as a Disciples of Christ minister. And he continued to serve as needed until his physical limitations required him to stop.

Joan and I with our youngest son, Bob

At the time this book was written, Rev. Harper, Joan and his youngest son, Bob were happily living on a ranch north of Harrold, Texas. They enjoyed the company of four miniature spotted donkeys, one horse, three dogs and one cat. From time to time, they hosted church services at a campground on the property. The beauty of the ranch environment was offered as a spiritual refuge for local churches as well as other religious organizations.

Introduction

I was conceived into being somewhere around the middle of December and took my first breath of great, fresh, Texas air on August 10, 1914. Dr. Riley, the family doctor, drove his horse-drawn buggy-rig with his chicken cage on the back, from Alvord, the six miles out to the Harper farm and brought me into the world; "kicking and screaming" according to Mama. After Dr. Riley left, she looked me over—I looked fairly normal, so she named me after her father—my Grampa, Oliver Miller. Papa never liked my Grampa very much so he always didn't like me very much either. The way I know mama named me after the doctor left is that the doctor recorded my birth in the archives at "Decatur, the county seat of Wise" as "Baby Boy Harper." Papa wanted another girl, hence the name Cleo. The Oliver Cleo Baby Boy must have been slightly over size. Mama never told me how many chickens the doctor charged per-pound to deliver me.

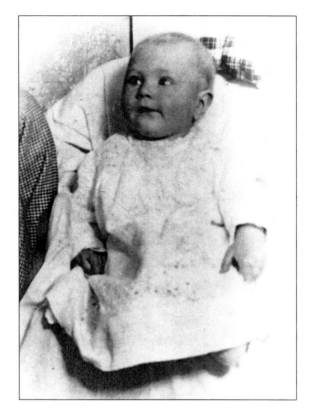

Baby Boy Harper

Papa wanted me to become a farmer. I dismissed that idea before I got out of diapers. Mama wanted me to be a doctor but after teething on a lead fishing sinker and eating lead based paint so that my brain rattled when I walked, that was out. Who would want a "*duh-uknow*" doctor doing their appendectomy? I wanted to become a real cowboy until I found out that real cowboys have to work cattle, repair fences, feed and castrate bull calves in all kinds of weather. Cowboys don't just ride around on squeaky saddles and high-stepping ponies all day. So much for that dream. Get a job, work hard, save money, invest and build a fortune—in the thirties and forties? Back then, your income would never—ever exceed your living expenses. I think there must have been a law to that effect. The largest salary I ever received in the thirties and forties was 75 cents an hour. The need for cheap labor was one of the reasons robots and wet-backs were invented. Minimum wages got legislated into being so that everybody would have to pay maximum income taxes in order to have enough government employees to fill all of those vacant offices in D.C. You see? Franklin Delano Roosevelt couldn't stand to see a vacant office. He also loved to pay good wages and great retirement income to all of his employees. Washington had to keep raising taxes more and more until everybody, opting for a government job, could be paid more money. Higher and higher our taxation had to grow in order to take care of our bigger and more expensive Government. Then came to pass the prophecies of brother Ross Perrot about *MORE TAXATION*: *"That sucking sound you will hear is jobs headed south across the Rio Grande."* How on earth could I ever create a fortune? I once tried being a business man. The result was a double digit disaster. I lost the mother-load, my temper, my savings plus much—much—more. That was when I decided to pray about the matter. I knocked, the door opened; there I found all kinds of riches I never knew existed, a wealth which there is not enough gold at Fort Knox to purchase. It is "The way of truth and life," the only way to the <u>top</u>, regardless of one's profession. Therefore, I adjusted my sails firmly into the powerful winds of faith; determined once and for all that the most needed of all professions in this deeply troubled world was Attitude Doctors. I began to finger the pages of *social studies* along with the Bible and the Constitution provided by our Nation's Founding Fathers.

My original design was to become a minister; so all of that seemed to fit together in a most telling call from God. I became truly devoted to such ministry for the rest of my days on earth.

My Grandmother was a teenager during the Civil War. I heard all about that war. Then, I was a World War I baby born in 1914; therefore, I remember that war in a very real way. Growing up during the great depression, the next thing I knew we had World War II. I am well aware that "wars and rumors of wars" (Mark 13:5-8) will continue until all the world can focus on the One God and Father of us all and we can govern ourselves accordingly. It was a great boost to our patriotism, when we read the headlines "One Nation under God" will remain a part of the Pledge of Allegiance. My prayer is for the day when all shall humble themselves at the foot of the Cross, that is the symbol of the Christian Way of Truth and Life. Read the above carefully. It is a thumb-nail sketch of the way we were. I will try to fill in the blanks as we go along. Some of the personalities that have inspired much of my writing and personal mind-set, I must warn you, are not all of the highest social order, but simple country folk I still find a part of my fondest memories.

The first World War was in progress when I arrived on earth. I must have begun remembering at a very early age. Picking up peach seeds out in the orchard, under the peach trees, was one of my first recollections about that terrible war. The peach seeds were to be ground up and prepared to be used in filtering devices for breathing masks worn by soldiers on the battle front in France. I have no idea how old I was then, but it rings clear in my memory; how proud I was that I could help in the war effort. Somebody must have impressed that upon my memory so strongly that I could actually remember how those peach seeds were to be prepared and used. It is still a mystery to me. None of my siblings, though older than I and helped in the same way, could remember this. I know I didn't dream it. History records my memories as being true.

According to history, it was September 1915 that a regiment of the German army under the command of Lieutenant Colonel Charles Faulkes threw opened canisters of chlorine gas to be carried by the wind into the British and French lines. Later, they used mustard gas, which was much more deadly. At first the Allied soldiers were given cotton masks to hold over their faces in the event of gas. The cotton masks had to be soaked in bicarbonate of soda. The soldiers soon learned that they could get the same results if they simply urinated on the pads. It was in 1917 that the army was issuing masks filled with charcoal from crushed peach seeds and what ever else would filter out the deadly gas. That worked much better and I thought, as a tiny tot, I was helping to win the war.

Other things I remember about that awful War was hearing people talk about the sinking of the Lusitanian. I can still hear, in my mind, the weeping and sense the awful fear that was being expressed by relatives of the hundreds of people who perished on that great ship. It was sunk by a German U boat in the North Sea, marking the beginning of the First World War.

LIFE IN THE VALLEY

Papa, Aaron C. Harper with his working mules (Jude and Red) on a cold winter day back on the farm in Wise county.

This is the way we were on Sunday morning, the first day of a new week, in the Lake Valley community where I grew up. There would always seem to be a kind of eerie calm in the air. Even conversations between family members were afloat in a haven of serene air. As a child, I was led to believe that Sunday was a time for spiritual cleansing. Saturday evening was a time for the old number 4 wash tub to be set up out in the smokehouse, filled with hot water from the reservoir that hung against the fire-box of the wood-burning cook stove in the kitchen. Another bucket full of cool water from the cistern on the back porch was added to make the temperature just right. It was time for the Saturday night bath. Summer time was better for my brother and me. We could take our Saturday evening bath down at the old swimming hole on Grapevine Creek.

The Good Book reminded us that we were to do no work on the Sabbath Day (that, to us was Sunday). However, there were always chores to be done just as on the other six days; milking, slopping the hogs, feeding the chickens, harnessing old Jude and Red, papa's mules and hitching them to the surrey. That was our transportation to the House of the Lord; that's what we called the old Baptist Church. The Church house sat on a wooded hill about a mile and a half north, across the valley.

Everybody dressed in their nicest, newest, cleanest clothes for Sunday school and church. We never went to The Lord's House in our old patched work clothes. We had to put on our nicest Sunday clothes and when we got back home we took off our Sunday clothes, folded them neatly or hung them lovingly on a nail in the bedroom. Mama would check them during the week to make sure they were clean, patched and fit to wear again on the next Sunday. Then, we would put on our "ever-day" clothes. I was never sure what we meant by "ever-day clothes" but we knew the clothes to which that referred.

The Sabbath Day also had some other pluses. It was time for hot, yeast rising rolls, mashed potatoes, thick-nin' gravy, stacks of fried chicken, fresh garden vegetables of all sorts; topped off with tall coconut pie or fresh baked crunchy peach cobbler, topped with real 'whooppin' cream. And of course, Iced tea, when ice was available. Ice would be available only a day or two after Saturday. Papa would bring back a fifty pound block of ice from Alvord. He would wrap it in an old quilt and put it on the back screened in porch. There, it would keep for two or three days. We would most always have one or more visiting families or the preacher and his family, if he had one. Sunday dinner was always special at our house, or sometimes a carry-in dinner (dinner on the ground) at the church.

I was the last of papa's four boys so his age may have had something to do with his being too busy to play with me. Most people can recall times when their fathers would take time off to go fishing, hunting or just for play time. At the old Harper farm there was never time for playing. It seemed to me then, and still does, when one gets so hung-over about making a living that he or she has no time to live, frustration may take away the sanity.

Papa once bought me a little red wagon. It was wonderful until I finally figured out why he was so generous with me. I must have been about six or seven years of age, and was getting big enough to start working. I could haul the firewood in for the wood-burning cook stove and large fireplace. My older brother Aaron had left home for greener pastures and there was no one left to tote the wood, so I got elected to do that chore. The instructions for all of the uses for the little red wagon would come later. It also came in handy when we harvested mama's garden. One could heap enough peas, beans, turnips or squash on the little red wagon to operate mama's canning activity for a whole day and into the night. It was absolutely necessary back in those days to have all of the many shelves in the old storm cellar filled with canned veggies before the winter season. We didn't have a Walmart or United grocery store nearby, like now. Come winter, if the canned veggies were not in the cellar they were not to be had. The same was true with meat. Suppose there was none in the smoke house, you could forget it. But, my mama always saw to it that we had something special to eat. To me she was the miracle lady, if there was ever one. Rest her soul. I still owe her everything I can possibly make of myself. She was a wonderful mother. By her example, she caused her children to realize how wonderful the gift of life could be, even in a world of stressful poverty. I did not know, then, that we were considered to be "poor folks" even by standards of the time. My parents and older siblings never spoke of life as being anything but good. However, there were some folks living in the valley who considered our family among the elite. We had a smoke house. It was a small, ten by twelve box building separate from the house, where we cured meat. We also used it, in the Summer time, for a bath house. It had one window on the west side facing out toward the road so that one could be busy in there and still watch for the mail carrying man.

Like most young boys, I dreamed about becoming a *brave fire fighter*. It was, however, a dream of short duration. On my way to the cow-lot one cold winter morning to do the milking, I just happened to look up on the roof above the back screened-in porch and saw the roof on fire. I suppose it started from an ember escaping the fire-place chimney. The brave firefighter, I dreamed of becoming, instinctively ran the fifty yards to the barn-yard watering trough and filled the milk bucket with water. I ran back and with one swift dash of water extinguished the small roof fire. I then hurried back to the smoke-house on the other side of the house, grabbed the ladder, which I knew was hanging there, leaned it onto the roof, and ran up to make sure the fire was safely out. Papa came along about that time and loudly inquired as to what I was doing on top of the house. Wasn't I supposed to be milking cows? I tried to explain. As usual Papa didn't have time to listen. He had something else on his mind. After cleaning up the milk bucket and doing the milking I returned to the house. Mama, rest her sweet soul, was complaining about the mess I had made on the back porch. My fire-fighting days ended with a sigh.

MY SAINTED MOTHER

Dora Ellen Harper

My mother would come as near filling the image of a saint as anyone I have ever known. She was faithful, honorable, dedicated and a most loving wife, mother and friend. As wife, she probably endured more verbal abuse than other wives. This is, in no way meant to denounce my father. More about him later. I slept in the two-bed bed-room that separated the master bedroom and family room from the kitchen. So, many mornings I would be awakened hearing my father berating her. I never could fully understand why. Hearing her almost silent sobs became for me a horrendous emotional experience as far back as I can remember. Any woman with less devotion and dedication would have packed up and gone back home before any of us children was ever born, but not my mother. She stuck it out *until death did them part.* My mother and father celebrated over 60 years of marriage.

Mother was a strict disciplinarian. The kind of love she had for her children demanded such. She never made idle threats, such as, "I'll tell Papa on you." It was a quick smack to the cheek or in extreme cases a peach-tree switch to the lower extremities. This kind of reminder was so very helpful to me when I was tempted to step over the line of family rules or defame the family name.

The old farm house had some convenient features that would not be so recognized today, but were special back then. We had a cistern on our back screened-in porch. The rain gutters around the back side of the house ran into a down-spout which ran under the house and into the cistern. There was a lever on the down-spout out side of the screened-in back porch to turn the rain water into an outside drain. It was always left to run the first water when it started to rain, to the outside drain. When the runoff had washed away the bird *doo* and dirt it was turned into the cistern. After a "big rain," the cistern would be full of good soft, clean rainwater. We could never afford a pump so the only way to get water was to draw it up in a bucket on a rope drawn through a pulley fastened to the ceiling above the cistern box. We usually had to strained the water because of the mosquito larva ("wiggle-tails" we called them.)

The Old Farm House (See arrow to locate the lever)

Cleanliness was one of her transforming qualities. Those were the days when wash day meant building a wood fire under the old ten gallon cast iron wash pot. It required drawing water from the cistern on the back porch, pouring it into a three gallon bucket (without spilling any on the floor), carrying it around the house through the orchard gate to the wash pot, emptying the bucket, and returning again and again until the pot was sufficiently filled. Then it was time to bring enough wood from the wood pile, which was located about a hundred yards south, in the horse lot. It was my chore to build a fire under the pot. The greater the fire the more intense the heat. So, the water must boil with great rolling vigor.

Now it is time to cut up some of "Grandma's lye-soap" in little slivers into the boiling water. When the water was boiling vigorously and the soap foaming up just right, the white clothes, sheets, pillow cases, towels, and what ever other white clothes to be washed were dumped into the pot one piece at a time with the old wooden paddle which was worn with much use and age. It was for many years brought into play to stir and turn the whole pile of clothing and what ever was in the pot for at least ten or more minutes. They were then scooped out of the old wash pot using the paddle and dumped steaming hot into an empty number three wash tub. Then, other buckets of water brought from the cistern were poured over the hot washed things. The tub was then placed on the wash bench in the shade of the old Mulberry tree in the back yard.

Next came the ***rub board***. The rub board was a corrugated metal surface fastened to a wooden frame about fourteen inches square with two parallel legs extending down to the bottom of the washtub. Each separate piece of laundry was then rubbed by hand, up and down, on the "rub-board" with a squeezing motion until they were spotlessly clean. And then they went into another tub of rinse water carried from the cistern, also a number three tub filled with clean water with ***bluing*** added to bring out a whiter whites and bluer blues etc. The items were then wrung out by hand and hung out on the clothes line to dry. While this was going on, the ***colored things*** were boiling briskly in the wash pot to receive the same treatment.

After a hard half day with the washing, somehow Mama managed to cook her usual delicious meal with the help of her two little girls and do the dishes afterward. The rest of the day and into the night was consumed by the ***smoothing iron*** heated to a scorching temperature in the fireplace in the winter time and on the wood burning cook stove in the summer time. Every piece of clothing-shirts, dresses and even under wear, all sheets and pillow cases were to be starched and ironed. How could she possibly, do all that every Monday? What a woman! There was no such thing as <u>wash and wear</u>.

It was many years ago before I ever heard about the world of dinosaurs. To me the whole earth was still fresh and everything was new. Mama and my older sisters were doing the weekly washing. It was a dry summer. Water was scarce. They were up at the stock tank in the woods, where there was plenty of soft water and dry wood for the fire. I was playing in the edge of the woods where there was a washed out place in a large sand bank. The wash had unearthed a considerable pile of kidney shaped sand-stone lumps about the size of, or larger than a soft-ball. All of them were the same shape and size. I sat for a long time breaking those strange rocks open. Inside each was a pearly colored smooth, hollowed out place containing a dark brown flaky material. They were all the same. I had no idea what I was seeing. I have gone back a time or two since to see if I could locate that same place again. I am sure now that what

I was destroying was some kind of dinosaur eggs. There must have been a couple dozen of them. I broke them all open. Why? I was just playing. I had nothing else to do. If I had known then, what I know now, I could have played like I was a "paleontologist" and kept them whole. What a treasure they would be! Like the "Giant Mollusk Fossil" I found at the bottom of a deep wash on my Park Springs ranch, I let them all slip away not realizing their value. The great plows used in preparing the land for Coastal Bermuda pasture grass covered it over while leveling the surface. The thing was huge with mollusk markings on each side and would have weighed over one ton. It would be impossible to find it now.

"The earth is the Lord's and the fullness thereof, the world and those who dwell therein; for he has founded it upon the seas, and established it upon the floods." (Psalms 24: 1,2.) I wish that I might have moved more slowly and have been, even more observant in my journey through this magic world. It is filled with exciting blips of by-gone centuries and many marvelous things yet to be discovered. How can it be possible for all those bits and pieces of creation; all the beautiful people who have lived and do yet live to be described with simple words of history or even conceptual art. The Psalmist did indeed catch a rare glimpse of what we look upon with minds dulled by familiarity. There is a creation story in every stone. There is a spiritual drama taking place in every human life. Paul describes it as *"—now we see through a glass, darkly;—now I know in part; but then shall I know even as also I am known.* (1 Corinthians 13:12)

Woodrow Wilson was President of The United States when I first learned that there was such a person. According to the political hype, he caused the First World War. He must have been a terrible president. According to the news media he was also the cause of the Great Depression. It would seem that the way to become a terrible person was to become President of the United States. I wonder; is that still true? Well, perhaps: Naaa, not really.

According to the Reverend Coke Drumigoole, pastor of the Lake Valley Baptist Church at the time, God caused the iceberg that sank the Titanic. "There was gambling, drinking and dancing going on, on that great ship". Shame on those rich sinners! My childhood concept was, in the end, they all got saved because the band played "Nearer My God to Thee" as the Titanic sank. Cool, huh? That sermon, according to Papa, was "a shore-nuff dandy." But, that was the way we were.

MADE MY OWN TOYS

I'm pulling Zula Belle on a sled that I had made.

O ne of the necessary lessons I learned as a child was how to cope with boredom. I learned how to make do with what I had at hand. My first toys consisted of ***spool buggies.*** I made them myself from empty sewing thread spools. My Mama had to sew all of my sisters' dresses, and my underwear and shirts. She would save the empty spools for me. I would take a piece of bailing wire, (wire used to hold compressed hay-bales together) poke one end through the spindle hole in the spool, make a short sharp bend up about an inch, then another bend half way across the length of the spool - up again about an inch and a sharp bend out to create a seat (another empty spool became the little man) with an outward projection for the tongue to pull it by. I entertained myself many hours playing in the sand in the shade of the house. When I grew older and became more creative my favorite toy was a hoop, a 12-inch band of iron used to bind wooden wagon wheel hubs together. The pusher would be created by a short piece of broom handle or hoe handle cut to a comfortable length, with a short length of a narrow board nailed to the bottom end of the handle. I learned that I could *turn the hoop right or left by slightly twisting the handle*. Such experience, building my own toys, turned out to be very helpful in my later years.

Also, I was easily duped. Once, when I was about seven or eight years old my uncle Mose and Aunt Vinnie Harper lived in Papa's sharecropper farm house. I must have also been an early riser because I arrived at their house one morning during their breakfast time. My uncle Mose Harper was pouring some white karo syrup on his hot buttered biscuit. I had never seen white karo syrup. The only kind of syrup I knew was sorghum molasses. Sorghum syrup was dark to maroonish in color. My curiosity was always a bit over the normal so

I inquired of him, "What's that." His quick answer was, "Castor oil." I ran home and told mama about Uncle Mose (UG) putting caster oil on his biscuit. Mama only laughed. Not too long after that uncle Mose died. My prognoses: The cause of his death? "Caster Oil."

Most people love a good, fresh, ripe peach and I was no exception to that feature. One day I was playing in the shade of a large peach tree out in the orchard when I happened to look up and saw a delicious, red, ripe peach hanging high up in the tree. I tried to climb up and get it but the limb it was fastened to was much too flimsy to bear my weight so I tried to shake it loose but it refused to fall. My drooling appetite for that peach started my inventive genes to click on. It would take a long broom handle to reach that wonderful peach. How to get it down without breaking it would require a little wire basket attached to the end of the old broom handle; plus a wire hook above that to pull it loose so it would fall into the little wire basket. My inventive genes soon had that peach picking tool together. I picked my special peach first. It worked so well I picked all of the ripe peaches I could find. Mama was so happy and pleased with me. She kissed me. What a precious moment to remember.

I was playing with my spool buggies in the shade of the house one hot afternoon when four grimy appearing men stopped out front and asked for a drink of water. I ran into the house, drew a bucket of cool water from the cistern, emptied it into a water bucket, picked up the family dipper and carried the lot of it out to the thirsty travelers. My first impression of them was that they were strangers passing through the valley. They all wore side-arms and one – the one on the gray horse, with the long beard had a 30-30 rifle swung from the left side of his saddle. I didn't know the name of it, then, but learned, as I told my brother about it. Each of them had a *poncho* neatly folded, rolled and tied behind his saddle. As they rode away, heading north toward the school house I remember thinking, "Gee, I wish I was one of them."

We didn't have news papers, telephones or radios back then so news got around slowly. It must have been a week or more later, Papa was in Sunset and heard the buzz about the Park Springs Bank being robbed by four men, one on a black horse, one on a gray and two were on bays. The report was that they took over $700.00, which back then was a sizeable sum of money. When I heard Papa telling Mama about it, the next morning, I knew immediately I had just assisted four bank robbers. I didn't know then, but as time and events passed I came to know I had witnessed the escape of the Younger Brothers, with money belonging to the people who lived around Park Springs. Back then, the people who owned the money would lose it, in the event of a robbery, because banks were not Federally insured as they are now. After two or three sleepless nights worrying about being put in jail for helping those robbers; I went to Papa and confessed my terrible crime. For the first time in my memory, Papa looked down at me and smiled. He then said to me, "Son, there is no law against giving a stranger a drink of water. You did a Christian duty." I slept much better after that.

DADDY WILLIAMS

Daddy Williams was a name I heard my father and older brothers use often. I once memorized a poem about the Village Black Smith. That image would well have fit my Step-grandfather. My grandmother, Bedy Jane Kierce Harper, widowed at a rather young age, married him some time around the late 1880. I don't remember him as a person but I was impressed by what he did, repairing wagons, buggies, plows, harnesses, making horse shoes and shoeing horses. I was born in 1914 so I could not have been more than four or five years of age but I remember as well as if it were yesterday his old leather apron. Actually it was more like chaps, the kind cowboys wore in the sage brush country. I was fascinated by his repairing and tightening old wagon wheels. He would take a piece of old native oak wood, put it in the vice, and with his draw-knife he would fashion a perfect *feller* to replace a broken one. He would then heat the iron rim to white heat in his coal-burning forge, which had a foot operated blower. Then with his long iron tongs he would slip the hot rim onto the wooden wheel. It would smoke as it heated the wood to an almost combustible temperature before he had it centered exactly. He then would put the wheel into a water tank to cool it. I can still hear, in my imagination, the cracking of the wheel as the iron rim cooled and shrunk to a very tight fit. The wheel would be as strong and tight as a new one.

The horseshoeing was another scene of great fascination for me. He would measure around the horse's hoof to determine how long the iron stock needed to be. A steel chisel and a heavy shop hammer would be used to cut the iron rod to the measured length. It was then nestled into the hot coals of the furnace until it was white hot. Then, with his tongs, he would hold it on his anvil and with his large shop hammer begin to shape it, flatten it, and round it out to make a perfect horseshoe. He would have to heat it, sometimes two or three times before he got it just right. A shaper was used on each side of the flattened top side of the shoes to make the square nail holes just so. Then he would plunge it into the water tank to cool. It would pop and sputter and make steam rise from the water.

His little shop wasn't large enough to bring the horse inside so he would go out under the old oak tree and put the shoes on the horse. With his back toward the front of the horse he would pick up the front foot to be shod and hold it between his knees and pound the nails in. He would take his nib cutters and cut the part of the nail that came through the top of the hoof and bend it back and forth until the it broke off. He had to be very careful that the nail didn't get into the tender part of the hoof. Then he would take a pair of hoof clippers and clip the hoof back even with the shoe, then take a hoof rasp and smooth the hoof down nice and smooth and round. I can remember a special saying that he had: "If at first you don't succeed keep on sucking until you do succeed."

I can remember exactly where the old Black Smith Shop stood. It was about two hundred yards west of the old Lake Valley Cemetery where Grandfather and Grandmother Miller are buried, only on the opposite side of the road. The old shop was across the road and back a bit east from where the cotton gin once stood. The old cotton gin was situated on, what was at a much earlier time, the bank of the lake that gave the village its name "Lake Valley." Sometime before I was born, a gully, "Grape-vine Creek," broke into the lake and drained it. I remember the drained area as being very fertile fields that grew tall corn and great cotton crops.

My very earliest recollections of the "Horse-less Carriage" belonged to mama's oldest brother, Uncle John Miller - a Stanly Steamer. It ran on kerosene heated steam which to me made a frightening sound. That wheezing, puffing sound it made would send me running into the house and under the bed. Uncle John and aunt Dena lived in Alvord. He was a jeweler who repaired clocks, watches and jewelry - like rings, lockets etc. They managed to visit us when the corn was at the roasting-ear stage or the peaches were getting ripe or the black-eyed peas were ready to harvest. They always just happened to have a few empty gunny sacks in the back of the car in which to put their booty. I remember one time when the pears were ripe. The pear orchard was about a quarter of a mile east of where we lived. Uncle John insisted that I should be forced to ride in the old Steamer so I wouldn't be afraid of it anymore. So, I was hauled aboard kicking and screaming, and someone, I don't remember who, held me on their lap all the way to the pear orchard. When they turned me loose, I ran all the way back home and hid under the bed. I must have been about four or five years of age.

I was big enough to start helping with the chores around the farm, when Papa bought me a little red wagon. I could haul in the smaller and shorter logs for the old wood burning cook stove and the much larger, longer wood pieces for the fireplace. My older brother, Aaron, had left home for greener pastures and there was no one left to tote the wood. I was appointed to tend to that chore. The little red wagon came with the instructions for it's use. It also came in handy when we harvested Mama's garden. One could heap enough peas, beans, turnips, onions, beets and squash on the little red wagon to operate the canning activity as needed.

It was absolutely necessary back in those days to have all of the long shelves in the old storm cellar filled from top to bottom with canned fruit and veggies, before the cold of winter. We didn't have a Wal-Mart or United grocery store nearby, like now. Come winter, if the canned veggies were not in the cellar there would be none to eat. The same was true with meat. Suppose there was no meat in the big salt box in the smoke house, you could spend a meatless winter and summer. But, my Mama always saw to it that we had something special to eat. To me she was the miracle lady. If there was ever one who could make a silk purse out of a sow's ear it was my Mama. Rest her soul. I have always felt that I owed her everything good that I could possibly make of myself. She was a wonderful mother.

I did not understand then, that we were considered to be "poor folks" even by standards of the time. However, there were some folks living in the valley who considered our family among the elite. We had a smoke house. It was a small ten by twelve building out back of our house where we cured meat. We also used it, in the summer time, for a bath house. It had one window on the west side facing out toward the road so we could be busy in there and still watch for Woodrow Wilson, the mail carrier. As I look back on the scene I have to confess we had a good, care-free life. That's the way we were.

Here let me toss in a couple of whats-its:

The "*dash board*", a decorative, leather covered, frame partition, originally placed in between the horse or horses rear ends and the passengers on the buggies or surreys. It served a very useful and obvious purpose; to keep your lap clean and dry. It is most interesting that the word "dashboard" has since been carried over into the automobile age only for a very different purpose, It became an instrument panel.

Gas Pump – do you know how that name came to be? Perhaps some of you might remember. My wife is only a couple of years younger than I and she doesn't remember, the old gasoline pumps. Back around the turn of the century and the development of the internal combustion engine, gasoline stations needed a way to measure out the amount of fuel for the purpose of pricing. Many of the old time automobiles had the gas tank under the front seat. It was not only a likely place for it but it was necessary for the fuel tank to be elevated above the engine so the gasoline could gravity-feed down to the *carburetor* —(the gismo that measured the amount of gas, per air ratio). The earliest stations had tall 30 inch glass cylinders atop a pump-stand with numbers up the side calibrated in gallons, half gallons and quarts. There was a pump handle which the attendant worked back and forth to pump the gasoline up from an under-ground tank to the gallons or fractions of gallons indicated - depending on how much gasoline you wanted, or more likely how much money you had to buy gasoline. When the amount was reached the attendant would take out the front seat cushion of the old "T," (or whatever) put the fill hose into the auto's tank, open the valve to the glass cylinder, empting the contents into the gas tank. The price was strictly cash, chickens or whatever medium of exchange you could come up with. There were no credit cards. There was a time when chickens were used like money. I call that: the chicken economy.

Grandmother's houses. The chicken house is in the far left. Her houses Were in Wise County and her chicken house was in Montague County. (From left to right) Uncle Moses Harper, Uncle Bud, Homer, Ray, Grandma Bede Jane and Aunt Vinnie.

CHICKEN ECONOMY

"For the *love* of money is the root of all evil," (1 Timothy 6:10). However this Biblical quote has never seemed to discourage people from their love for money; although I can still remember when there was little or no money to love. Instead of carrying her purse to the grocery store, my mama carried her chicken cage. A 20-pound sack of flour would cost "X" numbers of pounds of live chicken. One fat, *elderly* hen (too old to lay eggs) might purchase enough coffee beans to last a month or so. Mama did her own coffee grinding. The old coffee grinder that hung on the wall was almost worn out. I was always awakened, every morning by that grinding sound. If the chicken weight was more than the price of the coffee beans or what ever, the grocer man would actually give mama some "lovely" money back in change. She would buy us kids some peppermint stick candy.

Why did they use *live chickens* in our chicken economy? Live chickens had a longer shelf-life. However, chickens still had to be fed; kind of like paying interest or tax. Traveling salesmen coming through the Valley - all had a chicken cage tied on the back of their horse-drawn buggies or enclosed surreys. Doctors made house calls back then. They would have a chicken cage to collect their pay. As I recall, Rev. Coke Drumigoole, our Valley preacher, had a chicken cage in tow. They didn't "pass the hat" during church, they passed the chicken cage after church. The preacher would always be invited to some one's home for a full-sized chicken dinner. That was over and above his pay especially if he had his wife and children with him.

We also had guineas, ducks and turkeys. But chickens were the real medium of exchange in the Valley. The chicken house was the repository of much of our wealth. Thus a wise saying, "Don't count your chickens before they hatch." Mama always kept two roosters for a flock of hens. Eggs would not hatch out baby chickens if they were not fertile. Fast running roosters were of great value in keeping production up. However, it was necessary to de-spur the roosters so they wouldn't kill each other. We also had a family proverb to go with this chicken culture. "Shame, shame uncle Ben, he shot at a rooster and killed a hen." Young laying hens were like interest bearing notes; the more hens the more eggs; the more eggs the more chickens.

Back in the twenties and thirties there were not all the ready-to-eat goodies we have in our grocery stores these days. We shopped only for staple goods to create the home-made goodies. And with our chicken economy we didn't need money to buy groceries or anything else. Our medium of exchange for all commodities was chickens, turkeys, ducks, geese, eggs, cream and butter. For example, if you wanted to purchase a 20 pound bag of flour it might cost you one rooster, two hens and one pullet, plus four eggs. I remember well, a 10 pound bag of sugar would cost six pullets - (a pullet being a young chicken). A sack of salt was worth a dozen eggs. A gallon jug of molasses was worth three fat hens and one pullet. Ramsdale's grocery store in Sunset had a large poultry collection pen out back of the store. A poultry truck would drop by once a week and pay real money to Mr. Ragsdale for his chickens. I was told that he had to pay actual cash money for the things we paid for with chickens. Mr. Ragsdale must have been a business visionary. Apparently he thrived on the idea that made Mr. Sam Walton, one of the richest men in the world. Mr. Sam developed and enlarged the idea greatly. However, back in the 1920's there were very few articles one would find in Wal-Mart today. Ragsdale-Mart had everything from horse-collars to button-hooks, which would not be much in demand these days. But Mr. Sam Walton's chicken business grew into very large numbers. Millions of chickens are consumed daily, thanks to Mr. Sam. He also created better ways of raising, storing and marketing chickens and eggs. Mark Ragsdale-mart' system was not quite as efficient as Mr. Sam's.

There was little worry about crooked CEOs back then but we did have to watch out for foxes, skunks and chicken stealers. Those smart and smelly critters could sure play havoc with one's *nest-egg*. There was nothing wrong with the saying - *your chickens come home to roost.* That had everything to do with the safe keeping of the Montague County chicken economy.

We boys in the valley learned a new way to spend a cold winter evening of feasting and fun. The older boys must have learned from their older boy - brothers for no telling how many generations. Anyway it was considered to be all right: We would make a salt shaker out of a snuff can, stick it in a pocket. After it was dark and the chickens had gone to roost we stopped by the nearest chicken roost and gathered a fat chicken. We would pinch its head off and take it up into the woods, build a roaring hot bed of coals. While some of the boys were doing the fire thing the others of us would gut the chicken, make a wet red-clay mud pile and wrap the chicken feathers and all into a large red-clay-mud ball and toss it into the fire. We would then go hunting opossums, coons or what ever for several hours, then return for our feast of baked chicken. When the clay ball was broken and pealed away it would take away all feathers and some skin. The meat would be well cooked and ready for the salt seasoning and if you happened to have a biscuit in your pocket you could make a dandy chicken sandwich. That was not considered to be chicken stealing.

On one bright, moonlit night back in 1921 a would-be chicken stealer named Pete Cantrell drifted into Sunset with his horse and buggy rigged with a large chicken coop wired to the rear of his buggy. He had the malicious idea of loading up a bunch of Mark Ragsdale's chickens. What Mr. Cantrell failed to understand was that loading a bunch of squawking chickens in the still of the night was a bad idea. Mark Ragsdale lived only a couple of short blocks from downtown Sunset and just happened to be making a trip to the out-house about that time and heard Pete's fowl attempt at burgling. He ran through the house, grabbed his old double-barrel 12 gauge, loaded with bird-shot and made some haste in the direction of the chicken pen. He emptied both barrels in the general direction of Cantrell's chicken rig. You might imagine how quick Pete's old buggy horse would get the heck out of Sunset. The would-be chicken stealer took off trying to "get out of Sunset any-way-possible." Old Pete was making haste to crawl through the garden fence back of Ned Potter's house when Mark let go another double load of bird-shot. By that time Sid Fetchet, the county sheriff, who lived nearby, heard the shooting and quickly jerked on his britches and appeared on the scene and the rest is history—except that Doctor Jones (also the local horse doctor) remarked, "I have never seen a butt with so many freckles. It took me all morning to pick all the buckshot out of old Pete's rear end"

Speaking of four legged CEOs called "skunks," I remember one morning Mama discovered one of them in the chicken-house munching on one of her favorite egg laying hens. She didn't dare disturb it in the chicken house but waited for it to eat its fill and come out into the open. She called me to bring the gun and shoot the critter, insisting that I follow it away from the chicken house before shooting it. It started toward the barn and for sure it was going to go under the barn so I needed to get a shot off immediately. But about that time my doggy, Buster, came on the scene and joined the chase. Puuee! He smelled bad for many days but I didn't have to waste a shotgun shell or prod the sucker out from under the barn. Buster always had a stinking hatred for skunks.

RAINBOWS DO HAVE ENDS

I once stood at the end of a rainbow—really. It came down on a hill across the road about three hundred yards north-east of our country home. There was no pot of gold there but the colors reflected on my clothing as I moved from one color to the other. I probably was about 8 years of age, maybe younger. I actually saw it and stood in it. It was around about me and even more like I was a part of it. What a memorable experience. It appeared just as the evening Sun was setting after a rainy day.

It has been so many years ago and I still think of that hill as being a place of magic. I once found a number of smooth, black stones, about one to two inches in diameter on my magic hill. Curiosity got me interested enough to take a hacksaw and saw one in two. It was really shinny on the inside like very hard metal. Many years later I learned that they were meteorites, blackened by the tremendous heat build-up during their falling through the earth's atmosphere. I never thought of them as being of any value. That was just the way we were. My magic hill was one of my favorite places to play. Papa would plant corn on the entire 10 acres surrounding and including this special hill. In the hot days of summer the tall, fresh, green corn foliage was the perfect place to hide away. Fresh plowed furrows in between the rows of tall corn were cool and wonderful. Mama sewed all the family clothes then, so she had many empty thread spools which provided me with some of my favorite play toys. Buster, my friendly little dog was never very far away from me. If my Mama couldn't find me she always knew where I might be. All she needed to do was call Buster for his doggy lunch and note the direction from which he came.

My older brother, Aaron Harper used to have recurring dreams about a stash of gold being buried near a spring of water on the South slope of my magic hill. My father used to skim oil from the shallow eddies surrounding the spring to grease his cultivator. The oil seemed to be produced by the continuous bubbling of gas up through the sand as I recall. In more recent years geologists staked two places to drill for oil in that same general area. The locations were never drilled. I still wonder about my magic hill. It was purchased from my father by the United States Government back in the mid 1940s and is now a part of what is known as "The Lyndon Baines Johnson, Grass Lands." It has long-since over-grown with brush and vines and is a wilderness haven for wild animals.

SCHOOL DAYS

Me at 5 years old (left) and Zula Belle, my baby sister.

I t was a crisp September morning in 1921; the sun was barely up. It was the first day of school for one little boy named Oliver Harper. That was me. That little boy had turned seven years old on the tenth of the previous month. He was now a school boy who with his three sisters, Flaura, Zella, Pauline, and his big brother Glenn would get all dressed and wait on the front porch for the Gray twins, Ena and Lena to come along. Then they would all walk together the mile to the Lake Valley School House. On the way, they would be joined by the Rice children, Urban and Melissa (Adele was not old enough), and then the Simpkins kids. Tula Faulkner, a very dear person who lived only a few yards from the school house, would be out in her flower garden waiting to greet and welcome us. The youngest one in the bunch was Oliver, (that was me). It was to him that she directed her first welcoming words. "Well if it isn't Oliver going to school. How old are you, Oliver?" With an embarrassed shuffling I answered, "I don't know, but I ain't very old." Everyone laughed. From that time on I thought I was the village comedian.

My first teacher was a man named Hector Skinner. Heck was a slight-built man, clean shaven and neatly dressed. He made a large impression on a very young boy that first day of school. The school house was an impressive building to a boy who had never been out of Lake Valley community. It was a two story building. The junior grades were on the ground floor and appropriately the upper story was the "high school." That made sense to me. *High* School would be higher than *low* school. The steps leading to the second floor were back in the far left hand corner as one entered the building. There was one large room downstairs and a room of the same pro- portions upstairs. The first through the sixth grade were downstairs and the seventh through the tenth were upstairs. For all of this there were two teachers; a man and wife, Hector taught down stairs and his wife, Ethyl taught the high school classes. This may sound like a fizzle for a school but actually there was much to be desired in this arrangement. Each class, in turn, beginning with the higher grades was called forward for recitation, the sixth grade first, and so on down through the grades. The reciting class would move to the front row of seats. Each seat had a desk built on the back. The beauty of such an arrangement was that the lower grades would be hearing the higher grades recite, read, and answer questions so that when they moved up to the higher grade, they would already know the lesson material. It could be a great learning experience. Curt Harper (my father) let it be known to all his kids that if one of us got a "whooppin" at school it would mean another "whooppin" when we got home. Now, that is enough to cause one to walk the straight and narrow and block out all temptations to sin.

In the lower grades, the desk seats were double. Each child had a seat mate. My seat mate was a little Dyer boy named Jewel. I was a shy child but Jewel was more so. On the first day, the teacher instructed the little first graders that when they needed to go to the privy (out house) they were to simply hold up their hand until the teacher saw and asked, "Yes, what do you want?" Then they were to ask, "May I be excused?" and if the answer was "yes" they could rise, walk to the privy, and return as soon as possible or, they might be asked, "What took you so long?" Well, Jewel either forgot or was too shy to hold up his hand and pretty soon the shared seat began to feel warm and wet. It was sufficiently plenty to wet two pairs of pants. Jewel and I spent the rest of that school day with wet pants, both too shy to report to the teacher. However, when I got home Mama noticed right away. "What happened to your pants? Wouldn't the teacher excuse you to go to the privy?" "It wasn't me, Mama, it was Jewel. We sat together and I felt something warm under my seat and I was afraid to get up. I might get a *whooppin*." My mother must have had an informative visit with Mr. Skinner because the next day he made sure we all understood what to do under such dampening circumstances.

FROM HERE TO ACADEMIA

I graduated from the Lake Valley Grade school in 1929. My ambition was to attend high school in Alvord, six miles south and east from where we lived. One of the attractions I had for Alvord school was that they had a football team. Basketball was also in vogue there. I wanted to play football with the "Alvord Bulldogs" but I never had the money to buy any of the necessary wearing apparel required. The Alvord School bus came within a half mile of our house so that would be the perfect set-up except for one thing. That would require my father to transfer his school tax back over to Wise County. Our farm was in Wise county but all of our social interests were in Montague County, the Lake Valley community, so my father had transferred his school tax over to Montague County. Needless to say he refused to transfer it back to Wise County' therefore my schooling in Alvord lasted only one year and after that I was no longer welcome. "If you want to go to high school you can go to Sunset." was my father's final order. A long, five mile walk to and from Sunset every school day was not one of my favorite options. The school over in Sunset didn't have much of a basketball team and no football team at all. I would need to shake that one out and see what could come of it. I was already aware that if I ever planed to reach any social plateau higher than our Valley, my present altitude, I would need a college degree. What could I finally turn out to be without that?

I once wanted to be an inventor. The best I would have been capable of inventing with my present education would be – like maybe: a mousetrap, flyswatter, bowling ball, or toothpicks and somebody beat me to the punch on those. I recall once, watching my mother feed my baby sister (before sis cut her teeth). Mama would take a bite of mustard-greens, cornbread and ham. She would chew it well and then, with a spoon take it out of her mouth and put it into the open mouth of my baby sister. Sis just loved it. It was already salivated, chewed and mixed. She told me she had fed me the same way. "Just like a mother bird" she said. I thought that was a lot of trouble for mama. Somebody ought to invent a chewing machine and make baby food. Ho hum, Mr. Gerber beat me to that one. However, it turns out, if a mother was caught feeding her baby like that today, she would be hauled into court on charges of child abuse or un-fit mother. How times have changed. Our Child Abuse laws have messed up a lot of potentially great people.

The only hope that I could see for learning beyond the seventh grade, in those days was to join the military. I was deeply aware of a future of great challenge. The freedoms of this great nation were being re-shaped by the pressures of a society with questionable intent. **That's scary**. We must always keep in mind that we live only one generation from the pagan jungle. I can't help shuddering with dread as I hear the pagan drum-beats wearing away the magic of our once dignified Christian society. Have we lost our way or is this only a fantasy of old-age caught up in a change for the better?

What ever happened to honesty and truth? When papa bought the last 120 acre farm he owned, the man told him how much he wanted for it. Papa told him he would pay him $10 a year, when he could. They shook hands and wrote up a deed and filed it at the Court House in Decatur and that was it. When Papa sold the old land, about 40 years later he still owed the man $70. Now, that same deal would take one at least six weeks to complete with a stack of paper one inch thick just for starters. There would need to be two or three lawyers standing over the deal, drooling and cooing and making funny gestures. The price of the real estate would have to be doubled just to make everybody happy. My, my how times have changed. Now, here comes the funny part – In the grand scheme of things no body owns anything. When our end comes in this world we leave it all behind. Shrouds have no pockets. Funeral Coaches are never equipped with a trailer hitch or even a roof rack. Ever wonder why? You *aint* taking it with you.

MY CALL TO MINISTERY

Me at 33, sitting on my old Indian Chief motorcycle with my oldest son, John.

S unday School time was special to me as a child. My teacher was named Nancy Miller (not related to my grandpa). She was the only person in the community who ever held out any hope of my ever amounting to anything. She pointed at me one Sunday and said, "Oliver, you will amount to something." That maybe wasn't exactly what she said but that is what came across to me. As a matter of fact, I never remembered anything else she said but that has been stuck in my memory all these years.

The Lake Valley Baptist preacher was a red-headed, freckle faced, heavy-set gentleman named Coke Drumigoole. He could yell louder, shake his longer than usual mop of straight, red, hair more violently and stomp the floor harder than any other preacher we ever had. Some of us poor lost sinners referred to him as *Old Drum-Goozle*. He would never have needed a microphone. He never liked me very much, perhaps for good reasons. We, Lloyd Miller and I, once platted his old black horse's tail and squished watermelon juice in the seat of his buggy. That could have been his hang-up. He never was sure which one of us did it. I always felt guilty when he looked at me. I believed that was the Lord convicting me of my sins.

Coke Drumigoole was the butt of a joke that went around. The old Preacher with his big black hat, black suit, black shoes over black socks, in his black buggy pulled by his big black horse stopped to pick up a young man who was hiking down a dark shady road near Forestburg. The young man climbed up in the seat and the journey continued. The preacher, feeling the need to say something religious, said to the young man, "Son, are you ready to die?" It was reported that the young man, already feeling sort of overcome by it all, muttered, "Not if I can help it." He jumped out of the buggy, disappeared into the brush.

It always appeared to me that the old Baptist Discipline had a lot more don'ts than dos We were not supposed to play on the Sabbath; however I did manage to find a way around that one. I could slip off and visit one of our poor lost heathen friends around the Valley; and there were a few. All those who didn't attend the Baptist Church were so to be considered. It was a time of much fun, that is until the Sun began to sink in the direction of chore-time; then I would always begin to feel a bit sick in the tummy. It was nearing time for me to tell the whole truth answering very personal questions, such as: where have you been? what did you do and with whom did you do what you did? Papa had a rather dim view of those who broke the Sabbath Commandment. He was never one to spare the rod and spoil the child; therefore I was never spoiled.

My maternal Grandfather, for whom I was named; Oliver Miller, had a different view. He was a member of the Church of Christ and was firmly convinced that it was the Baptist, and especially Papa who would lift up their eyes in hell. There was to be no sinning at either house. Drinking booze and gambling were cardinal sins. Water, milk, coffee and iced tea were the only drinks to be enjoyed. Positively no accoutrements for gambling, such as dominoes, dice or cards, were allowed. Dancing was also forbidden. No sermon worth the price of the Sunday offerings was to be preached that did not present, very dramatically, the terrible fire and brimstone heat to be experienced in the sweet by and by, by those who perpetrated such ungodly and sinful behavior. "…their worm shall not die…" (Isaiah 66:24) has been omitted from the more modern translations of the Bible. Praise the Lord for that.

Once or twice a year the members of the church would gather for communion. All those who were members of the Lake Valley Church, present, were asked to stand until served with a little piece of bread and a sip from a cup of grape juice. All sinners and foreigners were to remain seated. That included visiting Baptists— those whose Doctrine came straight out of the pages of the Old Testament. I never really understood the "sheep and goats" theory, nor did I ever try. The sheep never seemed to behave any different from the goats.

There were strict moral boundaries for our social behavior in Lake Valley. The nearest law enforcement officer was the constable over in Sunset. His name was Luke Rhine. Luke had a unique way of arresting misbehaving drunks. He simply whacked them over the head with the butt of is old forty five six-shooter, rendering them unconscious, got someone to help him load the limp body into the back end of his old buckboard and hauled him off to the Sunset "calaboose". After they sobered up old Luke would collect a huge fine of, perhaps, two or three dollars, a promise to "go and sin no more" and turn them loose.

But there was still another law *enforcing* entity for what was considered to be criminal behavior in our valley. There were those weirdly dressed, incognito men in long white robes with a starched white cone-shaped hat which had a flap that covered their faces and necks, with two peep-holes for eyes. But one thing they neglected to conceal was their shoes. All of us knew the dress shoes each person in the valley wore because most of us had only one pair of Sunday shoes. All of these weird people seemed to be members of the Lake Valley Baptist Church. Apparently it was their job to enforce the "Baptist Discipline" a book containing the moral and ethical behavior rules for the congregation.

One of the Infidel families, the McFauls, that I loved to slip off and visit, lived over the hill on the banks of Panther Creek. They were considered to be rank sinners, because they did not attend any church, and even dared to have Saturday night dancing at their house; served hard boot-legged corn whisky and/or possum grape wine; that is, until one Sunday night in the wee dark hours after midnight, a crude, burlap-wrapped cross exploded in flames in their front yard. A hand-scrolled note secured by a rock on the front porch instructed those dancing, drinking sinners to vacate the premises by the following Sunday morning, and they did!

Beautiful spring days bring many fond memories. It would have been the spring of 1931. I was attending high school in Alvord, Texas. I had finished milking the cows early enough that Monday morning to run the mile or so to catch the school bus. The Lofton children were already down at the corner, where we caught the bus, waiting. It had been one of those soggy, rainy, weekends. The country roads were near impassible. There was no paving or even gravel back then. Finally, the bus arrived, and we rode for about two miles when the bus slid off into a mud hole and was stuck fast. "Goober" (his nickname, was the only name I ever knew) was the driver. Goober had to walk all the way back to where ever and get a team of horses to pull the bus out of the mud. While he was gone, he asked me to look after the children. There was a chill in the air that morning so I lead the passengers down the road about two hundred yards to an old abandoned house where they could be more comfortable.

My older brother, Glenn Harper, was a Square Dance Caller, back then and I had heard him *call* enough to be able to do some of the "Texas Star," from memory. Well, to make a long story short, I rounded up the boys and girls and had a square dance. It not only kept them warm; it kept them in sight. I first had to show the boys and girls how to do it. However, I made one terrible mistake when I called it a **dance**. My brother referred to it as **Swinging Games**. I found out why. The Baptist church fathers, back then had a firm belief that people who danced were destined to go to hell, no ifs and or buts. Well, those little kids could hardly wait to tell their Baptist parents that they had been exposed to this horrible sin. So I became branded The Square Dance Villain of Wise County. How would I dare to teach those children such a sinful thing? It's supposed to be called *Swinging Games*, stupid. "Round up eight—let 'em git straight—swing 'em on the corner like swing-in on a gate." (Like rap) There's nothing sinful about that ....is there?

After a long, long wait Goober finally came rattling down the road with a team of mules hitched to a wagon. We loaded all the children into the wagon and slowly headed for Alvord School. Goober would go back and drag the bus out of the mud while we did our school thing. He would have the old Chevy Bus cleaned up and ready for the 4 o'clock return delivery, hopefully.

School busses were not really great back then. They didn't have nice upholstered seats as they do now. They had one long 2 X 12-inch bench down each side and in the center. The benches were worn smooth. When the buss stopped, everybody went sliiiiding toward the front. When it started forward, everybody went sliiiiding toward the rear.

THE FIRST NEW DEAL

Grandma Bede Jane and her brother's family on an outing in a 1922 T-Model Ford.

I can not erase the images embedded in my memory of the "First new Democrat Deal" America suffered—after the Market Crash in 1929, under a Republican President. People were hungry and jobs were hard to come by all during the early 1930s. After President

Delano Roosevelt came into office it was necessary for him to do something spectacular, like offer a New Deal. A big Democratic bail-out seemed to be the answer. So the government Bail-Out money would start with little people, like farmers. They were not smart enough to tend to their own business so big brother would need to take care of them. Crews were sent out to go from farm to farm limiting the amount the farmers could produce. Papa had planted (estimate) 20 acres of corn. He was made to plow up 10 acres of it because his limit was only 10 acres. We had 10 acres of peanuts. He was forced to plow up 2 acres. We were not even allowed to keep the hay. The sorghum syrup jug was almost empty so he planted 6 acres of sorghum cane. The government allowed him only 2 acres. Cotton was the main money crop. Our cotton allotment was zero—plow it all up. O yes! Big brother paid Papa for all of that. We didn't need a handout but Papa took it. So much for that.

I did not know that the government was still in charge of farming until I decided to plant a few acres of peanuts on my Park Springs acreage in 1965. A peanut farmer who lived over on the Chico road saw what I was intending to do and asked: "Do you have a Government allotment?" I didn't and couldn't get one, so I didn't plant peanuts.

I still feel like crying when I recall the sad eyes of the dear old milk cows which had *names*—like *Lucile, Bessie* and *Maud.* The government men herded them onto a truck and shot them like some useless wild beasts. Hearing the sound of rifle shots and watching them drop dead—kicking, quivering and falling on top of one anther, was so inhuman and cruel. I have never been able to understand what on earth killing our dear old milk cows had to do with anything. We were never even to know the fate of the carcasses. I do remember that we were hungry for meat but were strictly forbidden to take any of the meat from those mass-murdered cattle. Some of the young cattle were fat, in good flesh. Why we were never given some fresh meat to eat, I have to assume, was another "policy of the New Deal."

Some time later, during the Great Depression, I can remember Papa getting some raw cow hide somewhere that still had hair on it. He used it to cover some of his old cane-bottom chairs that had fallen victim to too many sudden, bony-bottom drop-ins. Papa cut the chair bottoms from hides with white and black spots like Holstein cows. I thought of them as being from one of my favorite cows, which the government men shot, dear old Lucile. She had the best, sweetest milk of any of Papa's cows and had unusually large, long teats that were sufficient enough to milk streams of milk into the waiting mouth of my cat. I could aim the milk at my own open mouth and enjoy good, whole, warm, sweet milk on a cold wintry morning – yummy. Lucile was one of the largest milk-cows I had ever seen. I liked to think that my drinking all that great milk from her was the reason I was larger in stature than any of my friends. My size made my school days different from school days of my friends of smaller stature. I was never picked on by any of the other boys. And girls — Wow, they were all overcome by my tall, handsome, good looks and social charm—but—I was also very bashful—darn it.

MY FIRST SIDE ARM

L ike all country boys, I wanted, very much to bear the image of a real cow-boy, six-shooter gun, large black hat,—the works. I found an ad in a mail order catalogue where I could buy and sell Christmas cards and they would give me a six-shooter that looked real but would only shoot 20 caliber blanks. Grandma let me borrow the money for the cards, which I ordered, already knowing where I would find buyers for them. My sister, Flaura, and sister-in-law, Elvera, would purchase them for what they cost, so that I could repay Grandma. I had my real blanks-firing pistol free and made a holster out of some of Papa's left-over rawhide scraps from his chair seat covers. Then I found an old leather belt one of my older brothers had worn out and discarded, cut it to fit, put it on and was one mean looking dude. There was one box of 100 cartridges that came with my Christmas card deal, so now I could make big noises like a gun slinger. However, I made my first mistake by wearing it to school one day. It was a well known fact that it would not be exactly met with favor to wear it into the class room so I tucked it, (secretly I thought) under the front steps as I entered. Bernice Holloway must have been slightly later arriving at school that morning because he knew exactly "where" and "whose,"—come recess. He beat me to it and had it strapped on before I had time to retrieve it. But Bernice made one very stupid mistake. Viola Dyer, one of the meanest, toughest, prettiest females I have ever known happened to come by about that time and of all things, Bernice put the barrel of my new 20 caliber gun against her breast and pulled the darn trigger. What happened after that was sudden. I am still amazed. Viola's big hand-bag made a couple of circles and ended up against the side of Bernice's head. She must have had it full of books. Bernice landed about 10 feet south of ground zero. Miss Priddy, our teacher, quickly came to the rescue. She picked poor lil' old Bernice up and helped him into the schoolhouse and stopped some of the bleeding. It seems his hearing was never normal after that. One thing for sure, he never bothered my toy pistol anymore. One reason was because Miss Priddy advised me not to bring it to school anymore. What ever happened to my 20 gauge weapon? Read on.

When I exhausted my supply of ammunition (20-gauge blanks) I could not find any more, even in the mail order catalogue where I purchased my original deal. Jewel Dyer came to my rescue. He would swap me his favorite top, a hand full of marbles and one of his better pocket knives for it. Jewel had the idea he could bore it out to fit a 22-caliber rifle cartridge. All of the Ben Dyer boys were good mechanics, all except Happy;—Hap was more into girls. Jewel made a gauge from a piece of bailing wire, bent it to exactly fit over a 22-caliber rifle hull, found a metal cutting bit the same size, chucked it up in the brace, placed the barrel of the gun in a vise and started his drilling operation. It went very well on the first encounter but when he turned it to drill out the back end it ker'broke, split right down the middle. The boy mechanic was not to be had by a slight failure. He went for the bailing wire treatment, winding it round and round the barrel and tied it off real good. Not to be out-gunned he shoved a 22 shell into the chamber and handed it to me. Well, my mama didn't raise any idiots. I handed it right back to him and hid behind a tree. Jewel thought that was a brilliant idea so he also got behind a tree, reached around from a safe distance and **blaam**—he drew back a bleeding fist full of pot-iron and bailing wire.

NAIL BUSINESS

It must have been, about the year 1923; Papa tore down an old school and church house by the Pleasant Ridge cemetery, for the lumber. The old building had been built by Uncle Moses Kierce and was no longer in use so he gave it to papa. I spent one whole winter in my spare time pulling nails and straightening them for reuse. Cleaning the old lumber for building a cow barn and latter a garage for the T-model was a good learning experience for me, teaching me about the value of things. A bent nail had value. If I straightened it, it could be used again. I pulled the nails from a large stack of 1 X 12 X 10 boards. The 2 X 4s and trim lumbers were more difficult to clear. Papa sold some of the of the lumber for enough money to buy the necessary hardware for his cow barn and garage. We never threw anything away. Waste-Management would have needed a Government "Bail-Out" to survive. Value could be found in every-thing, even old tin-cans; they could be cleaned, the ends knocked out, flattened, straightened and used to replace shingles that had blown off the roof. The round ends of the cans could be useful for covering knot holes in floors and walls to keep mice out of the house or corn-crib. Nails were never so crooked as to be worthless.

In 1925 Papa and Mama took me and my baby sister on a trip in their new model T Ford to visit Uncle Will Miller in Comanche, Oklahoma. Uncle Will was a carpenter and had been tearing down some old WWI barracks buildings for the lumber. The ground was covered with crooked nails of all sizes. My business brains began to click. I found some large tin-cans, a bucket or two and began to pick up nails and stow them away in Papa's Ford. I must have picked up forty or more pounds of those old crooked nails.

When we arrived back home I was unloading my nail cache when Papa frowned and asked, "What are you going to do with all of those nails?" My answer: "I don't know, but I will straighten them out and maybe somebody will need them." It must have taken me six months or more to straighten all those nails. I spent most of my spare time, after school and any time while it was daylight and I had nothing else to do, straightening nails. Papa had found a two-foot piece of railroad rail and had it mounted on a work-bench to be used as an anvil. He had a light ball-penne hammer which was just the thing for nail straightening. He also had an old worn-out shop vise that was one his step father, Grandpa Williams, left him. It also helped in my labors of love.

What was I going to do with all those nails? Well, Oliver Faulkner, a fine old gentleman who lived between Grandma's house, and the school house had a smokehouse that had been badly damaged by a storm. He would need some nails. Will Rice, the crabby old goat who lived just down the hill from us, needed to do some work on his barn; he would need some nails. Some of the benches at the church needed a bit of tightening up; I could do that. After all the nails I had given away I still had plenty to fill the needs we might have around the farm. I felt really good about what I had done to make the world a little better.

TO BE A MECHANIC

I once toyed with the idea of becoming an automobile mechanic. After watching my uncle Jack tighten the rod bearings on Papa's old "T" it seemed so easy. Papa gave him $4.00 for about one hour's work. All he did was drain out the oil, take the oil pan off, take the two cotter pins out and remove the nuts that held the bearing cap on, file away a small amount of the top side and replace the cap, nuts and pins. He did that to all four rod bearings. Then all he had to do was reinstall the pan and replace the oil. I could do that. Papa's old stake-bed truck had a slight rod knock so I decided to tighten the bearings. I did every thing just the way uncle Jack had done them but for some strange reason they turned out so tight I couldn't turn the crank. I over-did the file thing. I was sure that if Uncle Jack had hit the cap with only two passes of the file, another pass would be better. O well, I could fix that. So I went back in and loosened the nuts about a turn. Bingo! It cranked up just fine but the knock was louder than before. I decided that being a mechanic was not for me. For some strange reason Papa got real mad.

Buck Wages, a young fellow who lived somewhere near the Shotgun Community was fooling around Alvord one day and stumbled onto an old Whippet that James Trotter had worn out and parked behind Grissom's Garage. Buck was sure that it was exactly what he would love to own. He saw James a few days latter, offered him three dollars for it and bought it. I am not sure about the make but I do know it was a Whippet Roadster, with wooden wheels, black spokes, with a top that let back and it was very beat-up. Buck spent the next twelve months fixing the old thing up and getting it to run. After he got the thing going he spent more time cranking than driving. When all of its moving parts got in sync, it would run. It had no muffler so it didn't purr, but sounded much more like a thrashing machine. It had no brakes so the only way he could stop it was to drag his foot on the ground. And it must have had a carburetor for each of its four cylinders. When the fuel mixture came around just right it had a much greater back-fire than it did a go-fire. That wheel-a-cious back-firing causes another memory to kick in. Read on.

My old dog, Buster and I spent as much time as we could *slip away with*, hunting. Every time I would shoot, Buster would run in the direction I happened to be facing when I pulled the trigger until he found what ever it was I shot. If he was not sure which way I was facing—which was more often than not, because I was a bit light to be firing that big, old, rusty, double barrel 12 gauge, It could turn me around with a walloping kick when I squeezed off a shot. Buster would then run around in circles until he found what I killed, if there happened to be a kill. Well, Buck came by our house one evening, in his patched up pile of junk, took his foot off the gas pedal to slow down enough to make the turn toward the Tomlinson place and his old Whippet let off four **bam, bam, bam, bam** — backfires. My dog, Buster, spent the rest of the day running around in circles. The way we were back in the early 1920s.

One "July 4th" has remained very special for me; more than for patriotic reasons. Really, the very first Fourth of July I recall specifically. My elder brother William Roy Harper, his wife Elvera and my little brother, nephew, Bervin (Red) had spent the Forth in our Lake Valley country home. They returned to Wichita Falls in the evening and by some twist of fortune, I was permitted to return with them. W. R. had an automobile of some sorts with a rumble-seat. Bervin and I were enjoying the usual hair-raising rumble-seat luxury. It was after dark when we were between Jolly and Wichita Falls. Our attention was drawn to, what to me was a spectacular scene, the usual (though not for me) Fourth of July Fire-works over Lake Wichita was in full sway. This country kid had never seen the likes. It appeared like a giant Moon *"turned to blood"* rose up and then blew up. This kid from the Wise County sticks readily recalled the Reverend Coke Drumgoole's sermon about the world going to come to an end most any night now and I better cut out this sinning business and get my heart cleaned up and ready. He explained how that the firmament would erupt with fire and all of us sinners would get all burned. I was about ready to split when it was explained to me what was going on. Whoopee!

LOOKING FOR EAGLES IN MY FAMILY TREE

M ama and Papa reared eight children. One child died at an early age. Florence was her name. She would have made nine children, five girls and four boys. Mama and Papa married September 22, 1891. Their oldest child, William Roy, was born July 19, 1897. Roy was seventeen years of age when I came along in 1914. The older birds were beginning to leave the nest about the time my mental facilities began to record these memories. My earliest memories of my father were those of fear. I had a great respect for him but it was born of fear. I can't recall Papa ever holding me on his lap. I remember one time he carried me in his arms. My mad name was *SON*. Papa could say "Son!" in a way that sent chills of fear up and down my back. He seemed to have never intended for me to be and since I was, he would make the best of it. So, I thought for many years.

Papa refused to make it possible for me to finish my high school education. After years of struggles and bitter disappointments in the

work-a-day world and business failures, I finally got back to the business of working on my education, as best I could. When I graduated
from college Mama was there for me but not Papa. I am the only one
of his children to graduate from college. Would he be there? One of
the saddest, most disappointing things I have ever experienced was to
know that my own father cared so little for me that he did not attend
my graduation. This literally devastated my already crippled ego. It
took me many years of searching to ever come to any kind of terms
with that reality. Why? How could he be so uncaring? Later, this
would send me searching the archives of genealogy to see if I couldn't
put this haunting image behind me. I made some startling discoveries.

Grandma Jane and Grandpa Joe William with first child, Uncle
Frank Harper (This picture was taken around 1870)

First of all I began to realize that my grandfather, Joseph Harper, was at a critical age during the Civil War. He would have been around sixteen or seventeen years of age. Somehow he never was in the military. He must have been a very troubled young man, who died at a very young age after marrying and fathering four sons, the second of which was my father. My great, great grandfather was a large slave owner, doctor and trader, according to what I have learned. My grandfather would have inherited a slave-driver mentality and without question he passed it on to his children.

My studies of conditions around Andalusia, Alabama where my father was born began to make some sense out of this terrible puzzle. If you can't have slaves to work the fields, have a large family. Use your children as slaves. They are yours. Why not? There were no child labor laws to prevent such back then. A slave driver knew that slaves must never be educated. A good and useful slave had to be ignorant and submissive. With this understanding I am now able to, at least have some measure of respect for my father.

There were many of my father's generation with a slave driver mentality. Perhaps some good may have come from that. It was the generation of their off-springs that turned America around. They fought two world wars and a number of brush wars to make sure our world could be safe for our cherished liberty. It is my belief that the best of the best are born of great difficulties. I grew up in the country. A small community of country people were my social motivators. There were, possibly 35 people living in Lake Valley. I don't know that anyone ever bothered to count them. All of them were good, honest, humble, hard-working people. But they also were far from being perfect. There were rules called The Ten Commandments that everyone tried to adhere to. Consequently there was no promiscuous behavior that I knew about. Although most—if not all—of them were ignorant, poorly educated sons and daughters of the generations following the Civil War. Children were destined to grow up and live much as did the now freed slaves of the Antebellum era.

Sunrise was a scene of families working side by side in the fields. Planting, plowing, and harvesting was the way of survival. A day in the life of people in those days is considered primitive by today's standards. Work, work, work! All else was secondary. Education was one of the least important issues at our house. If one could read, write, add, multiply and divide they were considered to be sufficiently educated. This was a definite step forward from the slave days. The slaves were not to be educated because the more ignorant the slave, the more they must depend on the graces of "Ol-Massa." The most useful slaves were those who were most dependent. Some of this "slave owner mentality" trickled over into generations that followed the Civil War. Knowing the history of slavery helped many of us deal with the-not-so-good father-child relation-ships of my generation.

Poverty was an attitude actually cherished and cultivated by many in the past. "Blessed are the poor in spirit" (Matthew 5:3)was sort of a motto for our fathers, therefore, riches were sinful. I can recall the cold, rainy, icy, early morning chores. We were to go out into the mud (mud mixed with animal excrement) ankle deep to feed animals and milk the cows. Our foot-wear consisted of darned socks and hand-me-down shoes, slippers or anything else we could find to wear. Most often the soles were worn out. We would cut a piece of cardboard or anything we could find to cut and shape to fit inside the shoe to cover the holes. Imagine the squishy mess that leaked into your shoes while tiptoeing through the barn-yard muck. Bitter cold and wet was a time we dreaded most. There was never any time off from chores. Summer, Winter, Spring and Fall the fear, dread and boredom went on. However, it is so true that the harder the climb, the more enduring the climber becomes. Reality most strongly suggests that "…but with God all things are possible." (Matthew 19:26) That is how things were when I was a child.

SORGHUM MOLASSES

B ack on the farm July would be time to harvest sorghum cane. We would use a machete to strip away the foliage from the cane, lop off the top–seed-pod and then cut the canes off at ground level. The stripped cane would be left lying on the ground where it fell. Next, a back-bending exercise would be gathering up the canes and stacking them on a wagon to be taken to the syrup mill. There, at the mill, the canes would be run between two iron rollers to squeeze out the juice. The iron rollers, about eighteen inches in circumference and a foot or so long were held together by heavy springs. The rollers would be powered by a horse hitched to a 20 feet long fulcrum. There would be another thinner pole extended ahead of the horse to lead it in a circle. The rollers would be mounted about 5 or so feet above the ground with the fulcrum mounted above that, in order to give the person feeding the canes through the rollers enough height to work sitting safely upright. The fulcrum would slant down to singletree height, about 18 inches above the ground at the outer end. The juice from the canes would then be caught in a pan suspended under the rollers and then through a pipe with a control valve draining into the cook-off vat.

The cook-off vat was made of copper. It was about 8 inches deep by 5 feet wide and 12 feet long. The vat had to be perfectly level. There would be a solid copper fence across the width of the vat minus a 4 inch gate in the end. These fences would be about every 8 inches apart with slip-gates at the ends of each fence — staggered — left – right – left etc. for the full 10 feet length of the vat. Below the vat would be the fire-pit. The steaming juice would be moved along by the syrup maker, using a pusher that fit between the fences with a heat shielded handle, from gate to gate down the length of the pan, as it thickened. By the time the juice had been control-heated and skimmed the full length of the cook-off vat it would have a beautiful bright amber color and correct thickness after it cooled. When all of that was finished we would have a supply of great *sorghum molasses*. Mama had a five gallon crock jug with a corn-cob stopper that Papa would take. It would be filled first and the rest put into buckets or fruit-jars to be given away to whoever might need it.

My Grandma, Bedy Jane Kierce Harper Williams

Grandma Harper always kept a small bag of peppermint candy sticks in her trunk. My sisters and I learned where she kept them. We would slip in, while she was asleep and help ourselves to her candy. We never thought of it as stealing. Grandma, I suppose, wondered where her peppermint candy was going and began to keep her trunk locked. She also kept her snuff in her trunk and my brother Aaron would help himself to her glass jar of "Garrett Snuff."

Grandma was about the only one at our house who had money. She received half of her eldest son, Uncle Frank Harper's, Spanish American War pension. His wife, Jewell, received the other half. Jewell later married Zebedee (Zeb) Kierce, one of Grandma' nephews. Grandma never liked Zeb for some reason. He was always trying to devise some scheme to take away her half of the pension; I believe that to be part of the reason. I remember one visit from Mr. Zeb Kierce. Grandma, Papa and Zeb were sitting around the fireplace talking and the subject of Grandma's inability to sleep without her whiskey and water toddy before bedtime. I remember Zeb made some snide remark about her store bought booze and promised to bring her some real good home made corn whiskey the next time he came that way. That was back during the days of prohibition. Grandma didn't take too kindly to his idea. Her reply was, "You do and I'll call the sheriff." Cousin Zebedee changed the subject.

My Grandma Harper (Williams) once made one of those post Civil War poverty dinners *Opossum and Sweet Potatoes.* It would be almost impossible to spoil a dish of sweet potatoes but that was close. As I recall there was most all of the meat dish left after dinner. My doggie, Buster, even turned up his nose at it. Now when I see opossum road-kill I notice the buzzards aren't particularly interested. What in this world did God have in mind when he created the opossum? Like the lowly skunk, it serves no known purpose.

PEDDLER MAN

Me, when I was 17 years old

When I was in my mid teens on the farm I was impressed by the Medicine Man and his fancy rig. He somehow managed to know about the time of the month when Grandma's pension check arrived. He had a wonder-drug known as Gerital that

Grandma just loved. The Medicine Man drove a sleek bay gelding to a shiny black buggy, with a large chicken coop tied on the back. The medium of exchange out in the country back then was chickens. Grandma was probably the only cash customer the man had. His chicken coop was always stuffed full of chickens by the time he got out to our house. Grandma didn't have chickens after she moved to our house. She only had money from Uncle Frank Harper's Spanish American War pension.

Gerital was highly advertised back in the Roaring Twenties. The advertisement pictured an elderly lady holding up a bottle of Gerital, boasting – "I once was bothered with stomach trouble but after taking Gerital I will put my stomach up against anybody's stomach." The recommended dose was measured in tablespoons but Grandma never bothered to spoon it out—she used a coffee cup. Apparently it made her feel much better. After her medication she could become the life of the party. She never learned to read. If she could have read the fine print, she would have known that it stated that her favorite medication was 90 proof—whatever that meant. It wasn't long after that, apparently the sheriff had a talk with the medicine man that may have changed his way of making a living.

I was not so much taken with the snake oil the guy was peddling as with his fancy fixings. He had a bouquet of peacock feathers sticking up between the horse's ears, shiny buckles and brass headed brads up and down the back strap, belly-band, britchen and tugs. The whip, standing tall out of the whip-cup on the side of the dashboard was tipped with silk lashes. It seemed so sissy to a country boy like myself. I wondered if maybe he might have lace on his under-wear.

I became so interested in the peddler man and his fancy rig that I decided to try my hand at becoming a peddler man. I was about 17 years old, tall, skinny, bushy hair, good looking (I thought), fairly intelligent, good, clean, moral, never arrested, no rap-sheet (that I knew about), loved and respected by all the neighbors except Will Rice who lived down the hill toward the Valley. I found a *want ad* in the *Sunset Signal*—the weekly news paper—wanting a *Watkins Man* to supply the Montague, Wise county area. It would only cost $17.00 to get started. I had fifty six cents saved up already and knew where I could get another fifty cents. The bridge across Grapevine Creek had washed out a month or so earlier and George Davis, Jim Harry's son-in-law, had contracted to build it back, and was paying fifty cents a day for workers. George was great among the folks in the valley, and he had played trumpet in the Marine Band during the war. I could possibly make a whole dollar if the job lasted long enough. I recall that I made more than a dollar and George loaned me enough to make up the required amount to purchase the neces- sary order to become a Watkins Man peddler. I could hardly wait to get home and launch my business venture.

In what seemed like a month of Sundays I finally received a large box of inventory in the mail. I eagerly dug into it to see what I had to peddle. As I recall, there were four bottles of Watkins vanilla extract, two bottles of cake coloring (red), baking powder, soda, several packages of jello, lemon extract and some other stuff I can't recall. I remember thinking, after I had sold all of that order I would have over twenty five dollars. O boy! I could pay off the twelve dollars and thirty cents I owed George Davis and actually have money to order an inventory even larger than this one. According to my mathematics I would very soon be able to have my own fancy Watkins peddler wagon. It would be so nice to have a solid black gelding with tan colored harness, sporting brass bridle bangs, all brass buttons, rivets, ham-knobs—the works. I must have stayed awake half the night planning my first day's run. Mama made me a large bag with a wide strap to go over my shoulders for carrying my merchandise. That would have to do for the time being.

I awoke early the next morning. Mama made me a great breakfast, as usual, then I was off to work. Walking was no problem for me back then. When my brother, Glenn, was away I could call Old Dick, my horse, but unfortunately brother was at home most of the time so, I would have to walk or run where ever I went—I walked. The first house I came to was the Loftin home. Jake Loftin had a large family and a very lucrative cash business peddling his *white lightning,* so I expected to sell a BIG order there. But guess what? I laid out all the merchandise on the floor before me and noticed Mrs. Loftin gazing longingly at the stuff, and finally informing me that she had no money. Obviously, her husband, Jake, was not generous with his ill gotten money. So I sacked it all up again and hit the hot, dusty, road over to the Dave Edwards home. Again I laid out my tantalizing fare and gave my best sales pitch. Again the word was, they had no money. I next ended up at Tom Grey's only to be told the same sad words, *no money*.

After a hot half day hearing those same two words I knew I had to either sell on credit or get me a vehicle to haul chickens and then, how could I cash my chickens? I came next to Jess Dyer's home, laid out my inventory and told Mabel to pick out any or all and I would sell it on credit – no money down—pay when you get the money. I guess I must have been the very first business man to tap into the credit system. It worked then just like it works now. She bought a bottle of vanilla flavoring, a bottle of Watkins liniment, two packages of jell-o, two cans of black pepper and a package of peppermint chewing gum. That was over eighty years ago. They are all dead now and there still is no money. The Dyer bill I did collect. Their son, Alba, was my age and we spent much time together so I guess I collected most of that bill eating Sunday dinners but there still was no money.

I took what was left over, after Mama selected what she wanted, to my creditor, George Davis and explained *"There is no money."* He understood, took the rest of my inventory and offered to settle the rest of my debt by my breaking and riding a fine saddle pony he had been given by his father-in-law, Jim Harry. I was delighted with the idea, that is, until I laid eyes on the lop-eared, jug-headed nag Jim Harry gave his son-in-law. O well, a deal is a deal and I learned early on that beggars are not choosers and one never looks a gift-horse in the mouth. I took on the saddle-bronco deal gladly; it was still better than walking every where I went. I called him Old Jim. He was not the high-headed, feisty pony I had hoped for. His best gate was a slow, bouncing fox-trot, when I could get him to do that. He was more like a "balky-donkey" most of the time but I was never in a hurry in those days anyway. Old Jim was too lazy to buck so he never gave me any of that kind of trouble. He would have been a fine kid pony if he hadn't been so clumsy. I found him to be about as exciting as one of Rev. Dale Thorn's Sunday morning sermons, but after all was said and done, I paid my debt.

PAPA GOT CHURCHED

Papa was a singing school teacher.

It was during the 1923 World Series, when the NY Yankees won their first W.S., that I saw my first radio. It was a big black box with a lot of dials and switches. It took both Uncle John Miller and my elder brother, William Roy Harper, to lug the heavy apparatus onto the front porch of the old farm house and set it on a table. Uncle John took the battery out of his car and hooked some wires to it under the table. Next, with the help of my three brothers Roy, Viven and Glenn they put up a hundred yard long antenna from the tops of some trees across the road and connected a lone wire from it to the radio. There were two pairs of head-phones. Uncle John put on one set of them and turned the thing on. He spent the next hour or so twisting dials and adjusting them just so. Finally, his face lit up with a smile and he began to recite what was happening on the radio.

Papa was not exactly pleased about the whole thing. First of all it was Sunday afternoon and they were not supposed to be doing work on Sunday. Uncle John, Aunt Dena, their two children, John Junior and Illa May had driven out from Alvord. They had not been to church. According to Papa that in itself was a sin. And here, dear Uncle John and my brothers were doing all this work to hook up that radio. It was too much sinning for Curt Harper. Besides all of this, Uncle John claimed that it was being done in order to listen to the World Series Baseball Game going on in New York City.

To Papa, hearing something that far away had to be some kind of wild assumption. It made no sense at all to him. I once heard him comment, "If God had meant for man to fly he would have put wings on him." He actually implied that his sinful brother-in-law was not being truthful about the matter. With this, Uncle John patiently plugged in his second set of head phones and put them on

Papa. He first had this what-the-h look on his face, finally he grinned and said, "I'll be darned." Well,—for the rest of that Sunday afternoon Papa never allowed those headphones out of his possession. He did let me listen briefly to one of the ear pieces. About that time Babe Ruth hit his first homerun and Papa jumped up from his cane-bottom chair and yelled—"Go Man Go."

One would never suspect that it would be possible for an old Atwater Kent Radio to split a church. Well – it did. A cantankerous old neighbor, a "good" member of the Baptist Church named Will Rice, who lived on down the hill a ways, between the Harper farm and Lake Valley, got all suspicious about what was going on up the hill at the Harper place. He first walked by on the road in front of the house looking things over, and then he walked on down the road a ways, turned and slowly walked back by and inquired of me what all this mess of wires was about. I answered all his questions and boasted that we were listening to the World Series Baseball Game. Mr. Rice went on his way back down the hill to his place.

The next Sunday brother Rice announced to the church that Curt Harper, the teacher of the men's Bible class was caught in the very act of profaning the Sabbath day and should be removed, not only from teaching the Bible class but from the church. Jess Dyer arose to poo-poo the claim as not worthy of such drastic impeachment. He, too, was immediately added to the list as traitors to the cause and invited to cease and desist. Well, things were getting a little steamy in the Lake Valley Baptist Church when Big John Miller (no relation) arose like a mighty thunder cloud, brushed his heavy handle-bar mustache away from his kisser and told Brother Rice how that the same door through which he had entered was still open and it would be well if he got the hell out. He did, but the steamy atmosphere remained. Many of the Rice fans were still sniffling and wiping.

Believe it or not, the Harpers and Dyers attended the Union Hill church (believe it or not—a Methodist Church at that time) for several months until the tears dried and the atmosphere cleared. The good people of the Valley decided that their church was not in the best of health without their Bible teacher and song leader. It took an invitation, and dinner on the ground, to nudge the missing pieces back into their places. Evidently the church folks of the Valley figured Sunday afternoon listening to a World Series Baseball game on the rad-e-o wasn't so sinful after all.

HARVESTING CORN

Harvesting corn was not much fun especially when you out-grew the "down row." What is a down-row? Corn was planted in rows far enough apart to be cultivated. For corn plants to have the benefit of all the nutrients and moisture in the soil it was necessary for all grass and weeds to be plowed, hoed, mostly both, completely cleared away. Early corn would be planted in June, or as soon as the ground was sufficiently warmed. Late August and September was harvest time for June corn. In more recent years corn is harvested by machinery. Some now even have harvesters that gather and shell corn. Back in my beginning the whole ear of corn, cob, shucks and all were pulled from the stalk.

With a team of horses (two horses) pulling the wagon there would be a horse on each side of a row and the wagon would run two wheels on each side of the same "down row." That row, being somewhat broken down by the wagon was more difficult to gather but being closer to the ground it was easier for a child to gather and throw the corn ears into the moving wagon. There would be two grownup persons pulling corn ears from two rows on each side of the wagon. The team of horses was commanded to walk slowly so that the harvest hands could pull every ear from it's stalk without stopping. Each stalk would have two ears. When the wagon was full of corn it would be pulled to the barn. On the outside of each crib (room) there was a window high up in the center. It was through that window the corn would be scooped up and thrown into the crib.

Each crib (room) had a full length door on the inside hallway. It was necessary to place a series of twelve inch boards across the opening from the inside to prevent the filled crib of corn from falling out when the door was opened. Hence a funny experience took place on one warm sunny morning involving Grandma's old buggy mare.

Grandma's buggy mare, Old Dutch learned how to open the sliding latch on the corn-crib door. I saw her one morning with her head inside the crib door helping herself to the abundance of corn. I made her go away and closed and tied the latch shut. The day before Grandma had received her pension check in the mail and was eager to have Papa hitch Old Dutch up to her buggy so she could go cash her check over at the bank in Sunset. She needed a glass of Garrett snuff, some peppermint candy sticks and to see if Dabney Drug Store had any of her tonic that was so helpful "for me shoulders," she reasoned. The Peddler Man who had kept her supplied with Gerital had, for reasons adjudicated by the sheriff, had not been by in a while and she was "plumb out."

Papa was always quick to fulfill her slightest command. He bridled Old Dutch and harnessed her up to the buggy and drove the rig up to the front of the house. Grandma climbed aboard and tapped Old Dutch with her buggy whip and away she flew. But things became a little wrinkled out on the road over about the Jess Dyer place. Old Dutch's all night corn lunch began to fester and produce an enormous bloat of methane gas. A resulting explosion occurred sending a squash of horse dumplings over the dashboard and into Grandma's lap. She had to turn her rig around and come back home to clean up the mess; and by the time she got home she was madder than a riled-up hornet. "Who left that corn-crib door open?" Why I received the guilty verdict I do not know, unless it was because I giggled out loud. That's the way we were back in the 1920s.

I once discovered that I could fly like Superman, only I could not fly over tall buildings. When I was about 17 or so years of age, papa brought home an old second-hand T-model, stake-bed truck. It, no doubt, had seen better days. It only had one door to enter the cab, the right-hand door. None of the old T-models ever had a door on the left front. So in order to open or close the door it was necessary to place your foot against the dash-board and stretch the door opening. My brother, Glenn, and I had been out gathering wood for the fire-place. We loaded some old tree-stumps that had been blasted from some newly cleared ground the previous year. They were seasoned and great for fire-wood. We had them piled high on the old truck. My brother was driving and I was the gate opener. I climbed over the door to get out and open a gate and rather than climb back over the old door as I would have to do, I climbed up on top of the huge pile of stumps. I popped my behind down on this huge stinging scorpion. I flew.

Incentive can cause strange happenings if properly initiated. I was in need of some money, which was not uncommon, then, as now. Selling furry- animal- pelts was one way to make a fast buck in those days. There was a large oak tree that had a hollow in it. That would be a great place to look for one of those wooly boogers. After climbing up on a large limb, nearly 6 feet below the hollow, by standing on my tip-toes I could look into the hollow. I found, to my surprise, there really was, a very large and a very grouchy old opossum in that shallow hole. That ugly critter reared up and tried to kiss me. Its snapping teeth barely grazed my chin. Now—there, I suddenly found myself safely on the ground. All I remember is that I did not climb down. I flew.

Surely goodness and mercy have followed *me all the days of my life* and I have dwelt in the house of the Lord ever since. (Ps. 23:6) Paraphrased-

I once witnessed a run-away team in Sunset, Texas that made the '*Sunset Signal*' (a weekly news paper). It so happened, that Buggsy Willingham, a young family man who lived west of Nickelvile, hitched his team of young fillies to his old surrey to make his weekly trip over to Sunset. Bugs had removed the back seat from his surrey so he could haul his milk cans full of *separated* cream to Sunset, where he put them on the train, north to a Wichita Falls creamery. He had arrived a little late and trains, back then, ran on schedule. Bugs had barely unloaded his cream cans onto the dock when the steam train blew its familiar whistle -whooooo-wt. Before old Buggsy could get hold of his young fillies the race was on. They knocked Bugs down and the surrey ran over him. It didn't hurt much, maybe a slightly bruised shin or so. Bugs jumped back up, – his pride all bent out of shape, and let forth with a terrible curse word, the likes of which the local paper, the *'Sunset Signal'* didn't dare print. It was too shocking. I heard what he said but I didn't dare run home and tell Mama. Buggsy wasn't ever known to be a religious man but he was fairly humble and never known to use curse words—out loud. Now that Bugs and his family are all dead; I will, with a feeling of guilt, reveal, the actual words he spoke on that occasion. "Damn it." Fortunately for Bugs, Mack Jennings was riding by on his speedy saddle pony, saw Bug's predicament and ran to head off the runaway team before too much damage was done to his rig.

THE DYER GOAT

The farm across the road on the west side of Papa's farm, once belonged to Tom Gray. After Tom wore the old land out he gave it to his son-in-law, the—*late,* Jessie Dyer. Jess Dyer had a rather dubious attitude toward young boys, as I remember; even his own two boys. He never liked me, probably for good reason. I often think about that strange relationship with boys that he had, in the light of my now pastoral, understanding of such behavior. Jess was a good man but so many good men have character flaws. Obviously he, himself, had been a victim of child abuse. His emotional demeanor was lacking in compassion. He actually caused the death of his two sons. I am sure he had no conscious intentions of doing such a terrible thing. His oldest son, Alba, was my own age and we played together as children. I was an invited luncheon guest at their house one Sunday noon. Their youngest son, Jacky, a toddler about one year old was crying. Jess had him standing on top of the swing-machine. He would shove the machine causing the little fellow to fall on his little rear end. When he would fall he would scream as in severe pain. Jess would laugh, stand him up again and cause him to fall and scream. He did that several times until his wife, Mabel took the child away from him and took him to another room. Later that week the child died from a ruptured spleen.

A year or so later Alba died from peritonitis caused by a ruptured appendix. Jess had made him plow cotton with a walking cultivator, on a hot day. He had a high fever and a terrible throbbing pain in his side. It became so severe he passed out and fell to the ground. His father then gathered him up, loaded him into his surrey and hauled him to a doctor in Alvord. The doctor immediately recognized his appendicitis and moved him to Decatur for surgery but it was too late. Alba died a few days later. God bless our loving memories of him.

Jess's wife, Mable was the oldest daughter of Tom Gray. Tom, was a rather unusual person. He fathered four daughters, Mable, Allie and his youngest two were twins—Ena and Lena.

It is strange how we so easily remember things that are of little or no particular value to us in the present age. For instance, the word commands to horses, Whoa (stop), Gee (turn right), Haw (turn left) Getup (go forward) Easy (slow), Ho (faster) Back (reverse). Tom Gray never used lines and bridles to control his horses. He always controlled them with voice command. His horses were well trained. Tom purchased for himself a used, 1923 model T Ford. He prepared a lean-to on his barn, a place to garage his new—second-hand T. The first time he drove it in he gave it the "whoa" command and it ran through the back of his garage. After that he made a door in both ends. He would open both doors so that if he didn't get stopped he would circle around until he stopped it in the right place. He finally learned to use the brake instead of the "Whoa" command. Stupid old Ford!

Jess Dyer, Tom Gray's son-in-law was over in Sunset one day, where someone sold, or gave him an old white billy goat. Jess was very creative. He made a set of buggy harness to fit the goat. Then he built a small two wheel cart with a double seat so that both of his kids could ride together. He patiently trained the goat to perform like a buggy horse. This would be his Christmas gift to his son Alba; a miniature horse and buggy; as it were. It is always interesting to notice how fathers often live out their own childhood fantasies through their children.

After all the patient obedience training and the cart painted in bright-colors all of the harness ornaments neatly shined, it was time for 'show and tell.' Since his eldest son, Alba, was my age it was determined that I would be the first to behold the marvelous gift. I still see Alba and his little sister Edna coming up the road with all the pomp and grandeur of some ancient charioteers. Wow! Now the exhibition suggests:—"won't that Harper kid be green with envy!" Well,—yes, somewhat, that is until my nosey, little doggy, Buster, spied the fancy rig. He, for sure, was not exactly delighted. This smelly old goat was not welcome in his territory. So, a couple of threatening yelps from my less than 'friendly pooch' and the race was on. Mr. Goat immediately forgot all about his obedience training, his harness bearing protocol and his horsy-like mission. He did a sudden left and sped off in the direction from which he came with my nosy pooch in hot pursuit. The sudden about-face, unseated little sister, Edna. She hit the ground screaming, jumped up and run after the fleeing chariot. The road, as usual was rough; I could see intermittent day-light between Alba's bottom and the seat. His constant yelling "whoa – whoa – whoa," could be heard after the run-a-way chariot was out of sight. The old goat refused to stop until he reached the safe harbor of home. After the storm was over I was relieved to see my lively little pooch returning. He expressed a wide, ear–to-ear grin and a patch of white goat hair in his teeth.

Several weeks later I was invited to the Dyer home for Sunday dinner. Now, I do not know this for sure, but I seem to remember that the meat fare brought to the table that day tasted a bit like 'leg-of-mutton.

THE TOMLINSON BOYS

The Jim Tomlinson family, neighbors to the east of the Harper farm was a family that impressed me somewhat. The oldest of Jim Tomlinson sons, Walter, must have had a good job in Dallas somewhere. He was always bringing his sister, Nancy, nice gifts. One especially nice one was unusual and a very entertaining gift. It was a "Phonograph," obviously a forerunner of the well known Juke Box. The phonograph was a sizeable box, about eighteen inches square and about four and a half feet high with a twenty inch turntable under the huge lid that hinged up and locked open. It had a rather sizable horn attached to a sharp needle. The black disks were about one quarter of an inch thick that turned round and round under the needle and produced audible sounds such as vocal or instrumental. It was of great interest to me. Nancy used to come for their mail. The Tomlinson mail box was on the same rack as ours and several other mail boxes. She would ask Mama for permission to let me go back home with her to listen to the phonograph. She had funny records of

"Mutt and Jeff," or "Amos and Andy." She even had some records with piano music and the Marine Band. I loved the big band music. She would play them over and over, per my request.

Sometimes her two younger brothers, Alton (Alta) and Brazos (Braz) would come in to listen. They were much older than I and I always felt intimidated in their presence. They were both tall, burley looking and I didn't trust them for some reason I never did fully understood. I interpreted their funny grin as they looked at me as a kind of put-down. There were other reasons that showed up in later years. The boys were just not very nice people.

My little fox terrier, Buster, was my companion as a child. We played together, hunted together and would even have slept together if Mama hadn't had such a dim view of having dogs in the house. Buster was a brave little dog. He would tear into any dog, regardless of size, caught violating his territory. The Tomlinson's boys had a large half breed bulldog that would outweigh Buster at least by forty pounds. That huge, mean old dog always accompanied the Tomlinson boys when they came to pick up their mail. They always came on horseback. Their mail box was on the same rack as the Harper mail box. The mail route out of Sunset ran in front of our house on the road that went through the Valley. Papa always called them the Tomlinson "boys" but to me they were grown men. Buster would always warn them and their dog about where his territory was and they better stay away. The Tomlinson's big dog would always grab Buster by his neck and shake him like a rag doll and almost kill him. I would cry and beg them to stop their dog but they would just laugh and go on as if it didn't matter. After their big, ugly, old mutt would finally turn Buster loose, I would pick him up, carry him to the front porch, bandage his wounds and try to help him get well. That happened several times. I would try to hold my little dog to keep that mean old mutt from killing him but it was always the same, Buster would slip away from me and tie into that monster and get all shook up again. I would cry and they would laugh and ride away.

I had to do something so I dreamed up a collar for Buster. I would make it of stiff leather and rig it with very sharp spikes. I found some roofing nails that were about one half inch long with big heads, and sharpened them to a pinpoint, then placed one of those sharp pointed nails about every inch around the length of the collar. That would give that Tomlinson mutt a very sore mouth, I mused. I had no way of fastening the collar around Buster's neck, so again it became necessary to do some engineering. How about making a hole in each end and use some bailing wire? I could even sharpen the ends of the wire. Wow was I feeling giddy about my revengeful idea.

Sleep did not come easy for me that night. I could hardly wait to see if my invention would actually work. Sure enough, the very next afternoon I saw the Tomlinson "boys" and their big dog top the hill in front of papa's old rent house. I went to work quickly to put my great collar around Buster's neck. Pretending to be holding my eager little canine friend as they arrived—I was actually reading him his rites, whispering—sick-em go-get-em baby. Sure enough, Buster did exactly what I told him to do. And so as the wicked giant folded his big ugly mouth around little Buster's neck, what happened was a great fulfillment for one happy, mean, little, old kid. That big dog let out a howl that was more of a scream and headed back east down the road with Buster in fast pursuit. The Tomlinson "boys" weren't laughing this time, only blank stares. I was the one whose tickle box was turned over. I rolled on the ground with laughter. When the Tomlinson boys came for their mail after that, their mean old dog hunkered down out in the corn field and waitedfor them to come back by.

LIONS ON THE LOOSE

It must have been the winter of 1923 that the ground was covered with six inches of snow; when Josh Bilberry was on the horn warning people to stay indoors because there were three big vicious lions on the loose. They were moving toward the south-west, according to their tracks in the snow. They would not be hungry because they had killed and eaten one of his yearling calves the night before, but they could feast on your children in case one of the children happened to be in their way. They could have possibly escaped from a circus; people could not imagine lions on the loose in Wise County, panthers – perhaps, but not lions.

The Bilberries lived over in the Newhart community south-east of Forestburg not far from Pelly which was just over the hill east of Grandma Harper's farm. Braz and Alty Tomlinson, neighbors to our east, heard the news with much excitement, loaded their hunting rifles, summoned old Bowser, their mean old dog that always tried to kill my little dog, Buster, and started out to capture those wild beasts, dead or alive. They had not gone far when, sure enough they came across the huge tracks of three very large lions on the Rankin's place, headed toward the Harper farm. It scared the stew out of old Bowser. He got one sniff of the huge cat's odor, and headed for home at top speed, tucked his body under the house and according to Nancy Tomlinson, didn't come out for three days.

The Tomlinson boys said that there was a big male cat and two females. Josh had spread the word that there was one female and two kittens. By the time they were being tracked in the snow on the Harper farm they had grown to one huge male, two females and several huge kittens. The larger extent of what I remember about those big cats is that they broke two inches of ice to get a drink out of the Harper stock tank, also broke the two top wires of the south fence and lost several strands of their hair on the barbs. I know; because I had to help repair the fence.

Three large mountain lions were seen in Montague County a few days later. The report stated: that there were three large males and two adult females. The Sunset Signal had the usual wise editorial that went something like this: *"Sunday afternoon Mr. Edwin McClure saw three large lions sitting on his front porch. Being afraid he would miss, he did not shoot his wife Essie. She was out there some place. They eventually went away because they were mountain lions and we don't have any mountains around here that I know anything about.*

The Tomlinson boys were tracking the lions by their prints in the snow all the way to Jack County. The snow-cover began to thin out near the large ranch country south of Jacksboro. Following the trail beyond that became a bit iffy. Gawking around in a mesquite thicket looking for tracks, Braz ran into Jean Hempstead gathering up some barbecue wood. Jean saw Braz first and hunkered down in some weeds, out of sight and shouted orders for him to put his gun on the ground and come out where she could see him. Braz realized she meant business when he saw her flash a little silver 38 six gun aimed at his vitals, and did as ordered. She sternly inquired of him, "who in the hell are you and what are you doing prowling around in my back yard?"

Braz, a little shook up at this point managed to reply, "I'm Braz Tomlinson. My brother and I are looking for some lions."

Jean decided the guy didn't look dangerous and for certain, sounded a bit stupid. She holstered her 38 and replied, "We don't have any lions around here. Why don't you go to Africa. They tell me they have plenty of em there."

By then Alty laid his gun down and came out in view and explained to the lady what their presence there was all about. She smiled and invited them to come in to her house, warm up and visit with her sick husband while she fixed sandwiches for them all. Daniel Hempstead, her ailing husband, had a bad back and was laid up for a short spell, according to his diagnosis. Jean came out of the kitchen with some of the best ham sandwiches ever to be created. Daniel remembered their father, Jim Tomlinson, from a time when they were both into shipping watermelons out of Alvord. The friendly conversation grew hot and heavy. Jean inquired, would they like some of her wine? She explained that she made it according to her Grandma Riddle's recipe.

Jean had gathered a wagon load of Parker County mustang grapes which she had stripped from their clusters into an old 20 gallon vinegar barrel, mashed them all up good, poured in a gallon of soft rain water, 20 pounds of granulated sugar, a half bushel of corn meal (she didn't have the required barley meal), half gallon of Mexican vanilla flavoring and the juice from two dozen large lemons. She was to stir well, twice a day for the rest of the summer. A couple of months later the mash should be well into a wild, foaming, fermentation. She was then to skim off the solids, squeeze the juice out of it and feed it to the hogs "a little at a time," strain out the dill-berries and set it aside for another thirty days to steep and ripen. Would they like to have a glass?

In the mean time Dan had hauled out the dominoes his son had given him last Christmas and cleared off the kitchen table for a game. The wine was brought out for sampling. Alty and Braz both voiced their approval.

"Would you like another glass?"

"Sure would" declared both boys.

Braz went bottoms up and moaned—"Shore is larruping-good."

"Another glass?"

"You betchie, that's the best damn wine I ever tasted."

"I'd like another—and another—and another." He finally noticed that he couldn't tell *which side of the dominos was the dots* so he believed he had had enough. Beginning to feel a little woozy, he wondered if he could lie down on the floor. Jean brought out a quilt and spread it on the floor and he plopped down and immediately got sick all over her nice quilt. Alty, disgustingly sober, wondered what to do next. It was dark outside and they were at least 30 miles away from home and on foot. "Would it be all right if we slept out in the barn?" "Of course it wouldn't be alright for you, our guests, to sleep out in the barn; you boys are going to sleep in the guest bedroom tonight," was Jean's folksy reply.

There were no bathrooms in country homes back in those days; so Alty took Braz out behind the barn and cleaned him up as much as was possible. The cold night air did wonders for him. The day that had ended badly took a turn for the better.

The lions were safely out of their reach by now. Besides, the Tomlinson boys had grown weary of their big game hunt and were ready to go home and settle down with old Bowser to hunt squirrels and rabbits. Sleep came sudden and sound. Braz was snoring lustily in jerky snorts as usual. Mrs. Hempstead's dog, Whitey was barking anxiously at something out front, Alty couldn't get his mind off of those huge lions – what if? About that time one of Dan's bovines let out a painful bellow (pronounced b e l l e r) out in the old corral, which brought the Hempstead's up rattling their artillery and firing up the old kerosene lantern.

They were all thinking "lions." It was as dark outside; as dark as-a-room-full-of-black-cats. There was no visible light anywhere above or below. It was dark. The night was still, all but the frantic barking of old Whitey.

"Those damn lions are out there eating one of my yearlings" Dan observed. "If I weren't so stove up I'd go down there and kill me a lion or two." He kept looking at the Tomlinson boys as if they should do something.

Braz finally raked up enough courage to load his rifle, open the door, walk to the edge of the stoop and return saying, "Sure is dark." Alty followed suit with his rifle cocked and ready to go with the same affirmation, "Can't see a dang thing out there."

Finally, Jean cocked her little 38 pea-shooter, picked up the lighted lantern and went out in the dark. She walked over to where Whity was circling a big mesquite tree, raised the lantern above her head and was heard to laugh loudly. This was followed by three shots from her 38; she came back, threw a dead coon on the porch and said laughing, "Here's you boy's big bad lion."

Alty and Braz gathered enough courage, after that to walk with Jean out to the corral to investigate the bovine disturbance. It was at once obvious that one of Dan's pasture bulls had arrived at the barn with the intent of taking over the breeding duties of his big prize Brahma. From the looks of the broken down condition of the corral fence the decision was short lived. The young pasture bull had distanced himself safely back down the trail.

There were no lions at the end of their long journey. Daylight, coffee, ham and eggs breakfast, goodbyes and the Tomlinson boys headed back home. The lions were never heard from again.

One Saturday morning I took my old 32-20 lever action saddle rifle and a hand-full of shorts (Papa wouldn't let me shoot longs – he was afraid I might kill some of the neighbors) and headed for the woods. I had never hunted over in the Tomlinson woods which was about two hundred yards south and across the fence from the famous Harper pear orchard. That wooded wilderness was like a rain-forest, only it seldom ever rained there. I hadn't gone far into that wild brier infested jungle until I saw something that was not supposed to be there. I stopped, levered a load into my rifle and aimed—and— aimed—and aimed but I could not bring myself to pull the trigger. That beautiful, fat, sleek, critter might be found in Jack County but not Wise County. I was looking at the largest, fattest, most beautiful bob-cat I had ever seen alive in Wise County. "O lord," I prayed, "don't let my little dog, Buster, see that gorgeous maze of teeth, and claws." But, as was to be expected, Buster did spy and made a run for the thing. That little mutt was not afraid of any living thing, great or small. Fortunately for Buster the Bob-cat didn't want to deploy it's savage equipment and ran for the nearest tree. It was hunkered down on a high branch but very visible from out a-ways. Again I raised the old Remington and pinned the sites on the coronary department; but pull the trigger? Un-uh—the old trigger finger just wouldn't operate. I tried to get Buster to go with me when I finally decided to leave the scene but he insisted on hanging out under the tree and holding his victim hostage. He was true to his nature as a hunter but he got home in time for supper. I told my bob-cat story to the Tomlinson brothers a day or two latter and even showed them some yellowish hair I found in the brush pile where I first saw the critter; to prove the truth of my sighting. They were real excited about my find and spent the next two years bob-cat hunting.

FARMING NOT MY FORTE

I now see farmers using large D9 Caterpillar dozers and huge eight wheel tractors that hinge in the middle as a steering mechanism—plowing and clearing out mesquite trees and post oak stumps. Back then we used real warm-blooded 'horse-power", the original horsepower – horses. A neighbor had a "stump puller" that papa could borrow. The stump puller consisted of a solid, steel beam, about four inches thick, eight inches wide and ten feet long. It had a 10 by ¾-inch bolt through the center width with a large steel hook on both ends on the same side four inches from each end. One hook would be used with a length of log chain wrapped from left to right around the stump. The opposite end hook would connect to a "double-tree" plus the two single trees hitch for the team. The horse-power would move left to right and twist the old stump out of the ground. If the stump was very large and unyielding, a two inch augur would be used to bore a hole under it and a stick of dynamite dropped in and exploded. That usually loosened it sufficiently to remove it, roots and all. It might still be necessary to use the old shovel and chopping ax on some of the larger, longer roots. The name of that activity was called "work—hard, back-breaking work." I know. I have been there—dun that. Many years later farmers could hire wet-backs to do those back-breaking jobs but back then there was no money to pay for such luxuries. If we could not do it ourselves it didn't get done.

Plowing the new ground could also be exciting. A team of horses (mules)hitched to a 14-inch, walk-behind, moldboard, turning plow wasn't exactly a fun job. That is especially true if you are 17 years old and bare-footed, which I was. Deep plowing with that big rig would be about 10 to 12 inches deep. In new ground you plow up rats, mice, scorpions, centipedes, snakes, lizards, gophers and once in a while a skunk. One time, and *one time only was enough for me*, I plowed up an underground bumble-bee hive. Old Jude and Red wisely headed for the woods and I was right behind them. Bumble-bees are fierce critters. If you are not familiar with those buzzy monsters, they are about the size of a tumble-bug and about as aerodynamic in general appearance but don't be fooled by their appearance, they are furious flying brutes with a quarter inch stinger and an accuracy to one thousandth of a meter. Once, if you ever get stung by one you will always remember where, when, the time of day, place and how far you had run to get away. It took Papa and me two days to get the old turning plow point straightened, the harness repaired, the swelling down and get my eyes open. Nope! No honey. They love to occupy old fox dens, in case you ever need to know their where-a-bouts. That is where I found them. Yes they make honey but I don't think you would want to eat it.

I did love horses so I found much satisfaction working with them. If you were working a team of good experienced horses they would help you turn at the corners by keeping the traces tight. If you were breaking a young horse to plow, it would be teamed with an older, more experienced horse. It would be necessary to slap the new horse with the reins to remind it to tighten up its end of the double tree. All of that sounds so primitive now. Just think, that would have been many years ago. Following a plow all day long; from sunup until after sundown with only a one-hour lunch break was no picnic. I was guiding the plow, doing a series of left turns at four corners; cutting 14 inches of ground, round after round until it all came together in the center. If one had a fast team he could cover 5 acres a day.

PEANUT HARVEST

One of the most challenging chores of farm life in the days of the horse-drawn implements was the peanut harvest. When the nuts were filled out to their fullest and the vines, which were fine cattle feed, began to turn it was time to harvest them. We would attach a plow, called the 'butterfly sweep' to the 'Horse-drawn leister' and set it to the depth of the deepest nuts and plow them up. The toughest job was to shake the soil out of the peanut clusters. We were good at shaking peanuts when we could shake two rows at a time and wind-row them, four rows piled together, for the pickup wagon to take them to a stack. The dust was terrible. The stooping was back-breaking misery.

Peanut thrashing time was more exciting. The Willets family in Sunset, Texas had a peanut thrasher driven by a huge steam tractor. Wow! That tractor was larger and heavier than the thrashing machine. It was much too heavy to cross the country road bridges so in order to get the monster to the location it would be necessary to make a crossing around the bridge. There were times when the huge tractor would not have enough power to pull itself up steep banks and horse teams would be needed to assist it. The huge tractor had a 20-inch *fly-wheel* on the right side and a long flat 12-inch wide belt made of leather to drive the thrashing machine. The thrasher was sometimes called a "separator" because it separated the peanuts from the vine. The tractor would be lined up about 20 feet *up-wind* from the separator or thrasher. Again, it was the dust that made thrashing peanuts unhealthy. Bailing the hay was also a dusty experience. Dust fever was not uncommon during peanut harvest. Some of the older men wore bandanas over their noses to filter out the dust. We, the then youngsters never knew such luxury. It was kind of neat after the peanut hay bales were in the barn to sit up in the hay-loft and eat peanuts that were left clinging to the hay.

I remember when Uncle Bill Kennedy, Burt Harper's maternal granddad moved out of the rent house, Papa filled it with baled peanut-hay. Peanuts left in the hay were a most delicious invitation to mice so the place was filled with the little critters. After the hay bales were all emptied out, papa had me helping him clean out the place. Mice were everywhere. One of them found refuge by running up inside of Papa's pant leg About that time a neighbor lady decided to come in to see what all the ruckus was about. Papa had his pants off shaking the mouse out. He wasn't exactly presentable to the lady so he asked me to stall her outside until he could get his pants back on.

Well, the lady didn't understand the nature of the problem and brushed by me and hurried to the rescue. Papa, by this time, having his pants at half-mast, tried to move hurriedly to another room, fell down, bottoms up, crawled the rest of the way. But it really got exciting when the little mice critters discovered the lady's long dress tail to be a haven for scared mice. First time I ever saw a flash of pink bloomers.

MY GRAYHOUNDS, TIP AND BABYRAY

Osie Lumsden, my late, brother-in-law and I were out with the grey-hounds, 'Tip' and 'Baby-Ray,' hunting jack rabbits one Thanksgiving day back in the late 1920's. We had walked a considerable distance; no jack rabbits, hunting on my grandmother Harper's farm, in the south pasture. A jack rabbit did get up at quite a distance away. The dogs saw it and gave chase. Osie and I were running, whooping and hollering as usual to urge the gray hounds on to the chase. Suddenly Osie was silent. I looked around and didn't see him. He had vanished. I ran back to where I saw him last and there he was. He had fallen into a gulley. He lost his glasses and was fumbling around trying to find them. Without his glasses he was blind. Osie was a really neat guy. Even his by-words were 'sweet.' His remark: "By-sugar, I lost my glasses!" I immediately saw the glasses and handed them to him. As soon as he put them on he climbed up out of the gulley whooping and hollering again. But by that time the rabbit had gotten into the woods and the dogs were lying in the shade. The jack rabbit won that race and I learned that Osie couldn't 'whoop' without his glasses; "By-sugar."

One cool Saturday afternoon, Baby Ray, Tip and I were hunting jack rabbits back of Papa's south corn field. The dogs jumped one of those long-eared jacks and the race crossed the south fence into the land leased to a man named Jake Loften. The dogs followed in an easterly direction into a thickly wooded area and of course there the rabbit ran safely away. Greyhounds run by sight only; they do not have a nose for trailing. While looking around in the woods for that elusive rabbit I was startled by a loud, gruff voice: "What the hell are you doing in here?" The voice belonged to Jake Loften. I had ended up looking at a mess of copper tanks and pipes cooking off a batch of Jake's high-octane corn whiskey. He was not pleased with my presence there. He had his old rusty shot-gun cradled in his arms. Although, he never threatened me, I couldn't get my eyes off of that old 12 gauge cannon, and was anxious to climb back over the fence where I belonged.

THE WET-DRY YEARS OF PROHIBITION

B ack in 1928 it was against the law to make and sell whiskey. "Prohibition" was not very well enforced in those days but never-the-less it was illegal to make and sell alcoholic beverages. The law frowned on the likes of Jake Loften's crude factory operations set-up in the back-woods of Wise County. Therefore, old Jake was concerned with my presence there. He knew that this Harper kid attended Sunday School and Church regularly and just might bear the knowledge about his unlawful manufacturing business to the wrong people (Although some of the church people were good customers). He was not pleased with my knowing the where-a-bouts of his secret whiskey distilling operation. Luke Rayne was the county sheriff and he just loved to use his chopping ax on the likes of Jake's whisky factory in the woods. Jake Loften must have gotten worried. On the following Monday morning Jake's whiskey factory had vanished. The only evidence that it ever existed were the holes where his "mesh barrels" had been buried.

I speak of Jake's moonlight production; illegal whiskey was often called "moon- shine" because most of the manufacturing took place at night, in some out-of-the-way place; hopefully the moon would be shining. A lighted lantern sputtering in the woods late at night just might draw the attention of un-welcome observers. That could be bad for business.

Saturday was Jake's favorite time to load his wagon with a fresh batch of hooch and haul it off to Sunset or Alvord to quench the thirst of his waiting customers. His was a lucrative business but obviously it was necessary for him to operate in the shadows. He had two young sons who wore <u>very</u> large bibbed-overalls with many pockets sown inside, out of the sight of the nosey public. The boys would load their pockets with the supply from the wagon and return for more when needed. They were deliverers of white-lightning created by the light of the moon. The price was.50 cents a pint and a nickel added if they didn't return the flask. When a likely, well known customer approached for a purchase Jake would motion to one of his boys to come. He always carried newspapers in his hip pocket. The single purpose for the news paper was to deliver the hooch shielded from prying eyes as he handed it to the thirsty customer. "Have you seen this article? Take it home and read all about it." It worked every time.

ORG—THE WINE MAKER

G rapevine creek ran north and east from the farm house where I grew up. It was so named because it was covered over by a preponderance of grape vines. Wild grapes were the substance from which a very fine wine could be created. It was Org Lancaster who took advantage of the free and plentiful supply of wild grapes. All Mr. Lancaster needed to make his fine wine was a large supply of grape juice, a 50 pound bag of brown sugar and a few days of fermentation. He next would need some old vinegar barrels which the grocery stores would sell after the vinegar was all pumped out. He would fill those with the new wine for a longer period of ageing. Org became an early entrepreneur in Montague County. He would pay us boys.25 cents a day to climb the grape vine laden trees along the creek, gather the grapes and drop them onto an old wagon sheet on the ground. His pay doesn't sound like much by today's standards but when I was a teen age boy that was considered fair pay in my native land. Think about it – four days - one dollar. A dollar then would be equivalent to about twenty dollars today and much more difficult to earn, so you thought twice before you spent it. There were no Government entitlements back then. If we wanted warm clothes and something to eat we had to work and earn the money for them.

Org Lancaster also grew watermelons on Denton creek bottomland. He didn't have to sell his wine to make money. On a good year he could make as much as $500.00 growing those great *Tom Watson* water-melons. Some of those beauties could weigh as much as 60 pounds. I have spent many days standing in the door of a boxcar catching and pitching those juicy giants to be shipped by rail to markets in the northeast. Usually I tried getting the inline position standing in the door where it was cooler. Pitching from the wagon or truck meant bending down, picking up the melon and throwing it in an upward direction to the catcher in the boxcar door. That was back-breaking work for sure. The ideal spot to catch and pitch was in the middle of the line. The packers were at the end of the line catching and packing the melons in loose hay to protect them for their long ride on a freight-train. That was a very hot two-man job. I preferred the broad door position because it was much cooler and the pay was the same. The in-line catcher-passers back in the boxcar had to endure the terrible heat. The temperature, back away from the door could become unbearable on some hot days in July and August. Farming and shipping watermelons was Jake's business but wine making was his juicy hobby.

I never knew of Org Lancaster ever selling any of his wine but when his wife was visiting her mother, which was often, he would have one more wild country fling-ding. The wine lovers from miles around would show up. How the word ever got around to all those drunks I would not dare to guess. The old crank telephones were available only in communities within five or six miles from town. There were no telephone lines available that far out in the back woods. So, when Effie loaded her three kids onto the train and headed for Fort Worth, somehow the word got around and everyone of Org's friends knew a wine tasting (guzzling) event was on, come Saturday night.

PAPA'S NEW T-MODEL FORD

Grandma Harper in front of My Great Uncle Moses' new 1933 T-Model Ford

I n 1925 Papa had a good cotton crop. We made twelve bales of cotton that year, to the best of my recollection. At $100 (more or less) a bale we had lots of money so Papa walked to Sunset, five miles, to buy our first horse-less-carriage, a Model-T Ford. Selecting the color you liked was no problem if you liked black. That was the only color they had. I shall never forget. We were picking cotton over on the north side of the farm and I would raise up every few seconds to check the road from town to see if Papa was coming yet. Must have been about 4 o'clock in the afternoon when, sure enough I saw that bright shiny black T-Model come chug-a-lugging down the road. Well, I loudly made the announcement and all of us cotton-pickers headed for the house. That had to to be the grandest occasion ever.

We all loaded up to see where we would fit in. Papa would drive. Mama would sit in the front seat by Papa and hold Zula Belle, my baby sister, on her lap. Grandma would get in the back seat behind Papa on the left side and the rest of us would hang on anyplace we could squeeze in. My sisters, Zella and Pauline (Flaura was married by that time) would sit on the back seat by Grandma. It must have been a tight fit. The seats were less than four feet wide. Glenn and I would stand on the running-board on each side, hanging on to the top for support.

The next day was Sunday. We were all dressed up in our Sunday's finest. I with my knee-britches buckled below my knees, my new silk shirt and tie and green felt hat, a present from my brother Aaron a few years hence. I took my riding position on the left running board hanging onto the top-support. We were going to church to show off our latest splurge of wealth. As we chug-a-luged along up the hill toward the church house at about fifteen miles an hour we came upon some of John Miller's cows out in the road. Papa commanded me to jump out there and head those cows back toward their house. Being accustomed to farm-wagon speeds of three or four miles an hour, I bailed off and hit the ground skidding on my front side. Old red clay, dry weather clods, were very hard and rough especially on my silk shirt and knee britches. I even lost my green felt hat in the flurry. The obedient son that I was, I fulfilled my good deed willingly but I must have looked terrible with torn bloody elbows and knees. When the task was finished and I at last arrived back at the church house, Mama noticed my beat-up appearance and inquired, "My goodness, Cleo what happened to you?" You see, everybody on board was so transfixed at the fast approaching road ahead that nobody heard papa's command or witnessed my golden deed.

THE ED GRISSOM STORY

There were some people in my childhood memories that I never considered to be role models or even persons of particular interest except they struck me as being a little – well not stupid but just a bit out of touch with reality. One such person was a man by the named of Edwin Grissom. Ed was one of the first auto mechanics I ever knew. He was a slight-built fellow, standing about 5' 6", weighing roughly 125 pounds, with a thick mass of blond hair that was seldom, if ever, cut, combed or washed. His every-day wearing apparel consisted of a greasy old Irish cap, striped overalls, a faded blue shirt and a pair of old well-worn boots. He actually dressed neater than most men did, back then. Ed could scoot in, out, under and on top of those ancient automobiles faster than a prairie dog can disappear into his burrow. He was, from his perspective, happily married, and the father of a pretty little blond headed daughter whom he literally worshiped.

Ed Grissom had a consuming love for repairing those old automobiles. He really knew his way around those horseless carriages, and even invented some useful items that made driving them, under difficult conditions, possible. For example; he created a cover to place on the front of the radiator for winter driving to help prevent freeze-ups. Water was the only coolant available back then for circulating through the engine to control the heat build-up. Ed discovered that kerosene substituted for water very well, if you could stand the odor. Not only did it smell bad, it was also dangerous. It could be combustible when it over-heated. One of Ed's most bazaar inventions was for breaking canines from chasing cars. Chasing after passing cars was a common past-time for country dogs with nothing else to do. Attaching a gunny-sack to the right front wheel was a sure cure. If a car-chasing dog sunk his teeth into that spinning mass of gunny sack it ended up in the happy hunting ground for naughty pooches. That was one of Ed's less popular inventions.

The other day out on the Wal-Mart parking lot, a lady with a new Japanese vehicle of sorts parked, got out of her car, pushed the red button on her remote, leaving her car with the horn honking and the parking lights flashing. She laughingly said to her friend, "Ain't no thief go'na risk stealing my new car. That anti-theft thing shore duz work good." This bit of pathetic humor reminds me of the days when cars were much less sophisticated. The anti-theft systems were much simpler then, but more effective.

In the beginning, motor cars did not have any lockup system, not even an ignition key. As car makers improved their product and there were more and more of them, they became more vulnerable for thieves to steal. Bud Goodman, who lived in the Union Hill, community was one of the first to be a victim of car theft in our neck of the woods. His was the only 1922 Ford around. so it was easy to find and return.

A young family man, I'll call Don Key who lived in the Scrougy community had harvested a bumper crop of peanuts in the summer of 1924. He decided it was time to up-grade his mode of transportation and bought a new Chevrolet. Chevrolet was a new motor car around the valley. It was invented by William C. Durant with the aid of a race car driver by the name Lewis Chevrolet; that would have been in 1911. It was a bit more expensive but Don was sure it was better. The principal difference between it and Ford was the overhead valve and the exterior magneto ignition systems.

Don heard about Bud Goodman's misfortune and was determined to do something to prevent someone stealing his new Chevy. He found a 10 foot piece of heavy log chain, wrapped one end around the front axle between the leaf spring hanger and king pin and around a huge old oak tree in his front yard, then sifted through the junk in his ancient tool chest his grandfather left him and found an old padlock he had once seen and used it to lock his chain securely together. I am assuming old Don slept better that Saturday night but when he awoke Sunday morning and realized there was no key for that old lock his countenance must have crashed. The rumor was that Don had to get Jim Augsburg, a lock and key man out of Wichita Falls to come out and unlock his new car.

After the Bud Goodman episode, people in our valley began a new fad. Bulldogs became the theft prevention of choice. Every car owner wanted a bulldog to train to protect his car. The dogs were taught to ride leaning against the motor cowling with their feet firmly holding against the front fender. When the car was parked the bulldog was trained to get up in the front seat under the steering wheel. That was a great theft deterrent but there were times when it worked too well.

Mr. Edwin Grissom saved enough money to purchase a new Maxwell. An oil man from Wichita Falls came through Alvord, driving one and stopped to buy gasoline. Ed become so wowed by that new Maxwell he simply had to have one. It was a two- seated touring model with a large trunk fastened to the back. There was a tool box on the driver-side running-board. It had a spare tire fender-well in front of the tool box. The top was secured on a metal frame-work, which could be folded back, if desired and there were side-curtains, which could be snapped on in bad weather, with isin-glass windows and a covered opening for the driver to stick his arm through to signal right, left and stop. For a right turn the arm extended out and upward, the arm extending straight out signaled a left turn and dropped downward for stop. It even had a thermometer on the radiator cap to register the engine temperature. The wheels were made of genuine seasoned hickory wood spokes. Tires were mounted on split-steel rims with attached lugs and according to the ad "Were so easy to mount that a child could do it."

The engine had eight cylinders. It was equipped with magneto ignition that had a kill-switch on the dashboard and there were brass priming cups for each of the eight cylinders. When doing a cold start it was easy to fill each of the cups with gas from the large squirt can (provided), then open all eight priming cup valves, stick the crank into the crankshaft cup, turn the motor over a couple of times, close the eight priming valves, open the kill-switch, spin the crank over and it was supposed to start. If it didn't start it was time to do the routine again, patiently, until it did start. Ed caught the train to Fort Worth, bought his new Maxwell and came slowly back home. The instructions for the *break-in driving* orders, were that it was not to be driven faster than 20 miles an hour for the first 500 miles. When Ed parked that new, shiny Maxwell on main street in Alvord it was like Ringling Brothers Circus had come to town. All of the town folks gathered around. You could hear the ahs and oohs all the way to Rhine's furniture store and mortuary.

Ed already owned his anti-theft dog, a 40 pound bulldog that must have been at least 12 or more years of age. He was a puppy when Gracie, his daughter was in the fifth grade. Old Bull (a likely name) used to walk with her to school, go back home and when school turned out in the afternoon he would go meet her and walk with her back home. He was white with black spots, well trimmed; his tail was cut down to about one inch long and his ears were shaped to a point from the outside toward the center of his broad head. He was a fierce looking critter.

Bull was already watching after Ed's old Chevrolet roadster. He was for real; so much so that if some unsuspecting stranger happened to get too near he would bare his big teeth and rumble a warning which was sufficient to cause the intruder to move on. Like Ed, old Bull was immediately attracted to the new Max because it had wider, padded seats. He claimed *squatter rights* to the front seat and only people with his permission were allowed in, all others were trespassers. He only left his royal throne to eat and tend to private matters. That new Maxwell was his responsibility to protect come hell or high water, meaning that if his territory was threatened he could be meaner than the proverbial *junkyard dog*.

Buck Spalding took Saturday off to drag his 1924 Whippet in for Ed to doctor it back to health. A winter or so back a freeze-up practically destroyed the radiator and Ed had ordered one from the factory. The old Whip had been sitting idle in Buck's hay-barn ever since, so it had been a haven for several generations of rats. Ed cleared out most of the rat nests and installed the new radiator, flushed out the gas tank, changed the oil, cleared the carburetor, filled the new radiator with water, pumped in a couple of gallons of gas and cranked it up for the first time in years. When all the rat-left-over's heated up, you could smell the thing clear across the street in Oak Dabney's drug store. Ed didn't mind, he had received the anti-blessings of the town neighbor on many smoky occasions. Anyway, he didn't have time for all the repercussions of his less than favorable operation. His daughter was getting married at 2 o'clock at the First Baptist Church and he had to be there for his fatherly duty of giving the bride away, so he cranked up his new Maxwell, woke old bull up, pushed him over and slowly drove home.

Ed's wife, and Gracie, his bride-to-be daughter, were already at the church getting all primped and primed for the ceremony to be. Ed, short on time as usual, prepared for himself a hot bath, washed his hair, shaved, brushed and spied a bottle of toilet water his wife had left unguarded on her dressing table and splashed on a generous amount. His wife had laid out his clean underwear, pleated white shirt, white snap-on bowtie, his old swallow-tail tux, with the stripped pants, cummerbund – all clean, pressed and spiffy, his freshly shined shoes and spats. The gold in his old cuff-links and studs had become a little bit tarnished but not too bad. It was the first time he had been all cuffed and studded up since his high school graduation and marriage to Effie.

Ed, all dressed up in his finest saw himself in the full-length mirror on the closet door, flashed a smile and did a huchey-cuchey wobble, put on his derby hat and headed for his new Maxwell. He stuck in the crank and Max started with one short turn, put on his white gloves, stepped up on the tool-box to take his seat, when his *theft protecting alarm* stopped him cold. Old Bull was not acquainted with this dude in the funny hat, smelling like a girl. Mr. Grissom was met with a whole face full of teeth and a guttural rumble that would remind one of an approaching tornado. Ed had the wisdom to back off. He tried to persuade old Bull to let him turn the motor off but to no avail. He made one final effort with a broom handle to trip the kill-switch.

In the mean time, the wedding had been put on hold, waiting for the father of the bride to appear. The future father-in-law-to-be was not to be put down in his own family affair. He hurried back into the house, took off the fancy wears, put on his smelly work clothes and this time found favor with old Bull and hurried on to the church. He came to a stop in front of, of all things, the groom's T- model Ford coup all ready, adorned for the honey-moon exit, with a long string of tin-cans and just married art work. Ed had his new Max parked smack-dab in the way. If that wasn't enough to furrow his brow - he was yet to be confronted by still another, more unsettling crisis. He was met at the door of the church by a wife and mother of the bride who was madder than a gut-shot grizzly, a bride to-be in tears and a preacher literally oozing with a sermon on the sin of "not getting to the church on time." A calm finally settled in when the decision was reached to omit the part of the ceremony that asked, "Who givith this woman?" Ed was seated behind the bride's family and the organist finally got the nod to commence "Here comes the bride." According to Ed, none of his family spoke to him for three weeks after the wedding, except his new son-in-law. He loved everything about it. With a father-in-law like Ed he could screw-up royally without disfavor

GOLDEN DEEDS

My Sunday School Teacher, Nancy Miller, was always talking about how we all ought to do a golden deed for someone every day. A friend of mine and I planned on slipping away to go swimming on Sunday afternoon. Aus Hand's nephew was visiting his uncle who lived nearby and wanted to go with us. We were glad to have him. He was a city kid but seemed to fit in very well. The swimming hole we planned to swim in actually was a cold, deep, living spring in the bottom of a very deep, treacherous ravine. The path by which we arrived was on the deep end of the long pool with high banks on both sides. It was about forty feet before the pool began to grade up to shallow. It was necessary that we dress down to our skinnies at the deep end, dive in and swim to the shallow end. That was the only way to arrive there. My friend and I dived into the cold, deep, spring water, swam to the shallow end and sat on the side of the pool. The visiting Hand kid dressed down but was sitting on the bank of the deep end. We urged him to come on in but he held back. We finally laughingly called him a piker. With that challenge he jumped in. Soon we were aware that he could not swim. He came up once fighting the water and the next effort he came only a part way up and then he settled to the bottom of the clear water in a sitting position and I saw his head slump over. I knew that he was drowning. We had to do something quickly.

I remembered once visiting my nephew in Wichita Fall and attending a Boy Scout meeting with him at the Southside Baptist Church. The subject that evening was saving drowning victims, how to rescue them and what to do after pulling the victim out of the water. The water was at least ten feet deep where the kid had stopped and he was back near the far bank. I remembered the idea that the victim would start reaching for me as soon as I lifted him up. I reached my long right arm as far out as I could and carefully gripped his arm as close to his shoulder as possible and held him at that distance until I had him in shallow water. Then I remembered how to lay him face down with his feet higher than his head and pump the water out of his lungs. A lot of water ran out of his mouth and he started fighting to get up. My friend held him down and I pumped some more. We finally let him up and he survived in spite of the treatment.

The Hand kid didn't want us to tell anybody. He didn't want Uncle Aus to know. But I couldn't wait to tell Mama about it. I knew she would be so proud of my golden deed. Mama wrote the Lake Valley news for the Sunset Signal. Guess what happened?

I left the home place in the valley about 1:30 p.m. one hot Summer day in 1931to catch the 2:30 train west. It (the old steam freight train) always stopped at the Francis Switch located about two or three miles west of Alvord to take on water, on or about 2:30 p.m. every day. I arrived just a few minutes early but old number 49 was already lumbering down the track, braking for the water stop. There, waiting at the crossing, was old man Ed Willet from Nickel Ville. He was in his topless buggy with his old red mule in the harness, returning from a visit with his brother in Pelly. It seems Old-Red, Mr. Willet's old mule was not exactly comfortable with the looks of that big puffing steam engine. He did a sudden bout- face, spinning the old four wheeler around, spilling big Ed out in the sand on his big, fat fanny. I hurried over to do my golden deed, but by the time I was in place Mr. Ed was already up cursing – "That dad-derned stink-in-ol-mule." Old Red and buggy were all hung up in the middle of a huge briar patch on the other side of the road.

A part of my golden deed then had to be getting old Red out of the briar patch and Mr. Ed dusted off and on his way. I should have received a huge gold star. That was a sizable golden deed. But by the time I had finished doing my golden deed Old 49 had finished watering and was rolling much too fast for safe boarding. I missed my train ride to Wichita Falls that day but I chalked up one golden deed. I was all set for the next time I went to Sunday school to tell Miss Nancy about my golden deed doings. She didn't give me a chance to tell about it. Blabbering old teach! I told Mama about it, and she sure was so proud of me. I didn't tell Papa because I was supposed to have been out following a plow that afternoon. I have often wondered why Papa was so crabby with me. It just maybe? Nah.

BUTTON HOOKS AND CORSITS

Not many of you will remember the simple little button-hook of the nineteenth and early 20th centuries. Those were the days when the button-up corsets, shoes and spats were in vogue. The ladies strived for the "wasp-waist" look: that is, really skinny in the middle and large below and above. They loved the old button-up corsets. Some of the less-petite women had to put a lot of pizzazz into their corset stretching, with it's string of buttons and loops up and down the back, to get the desired look; hence the useful little button-hook. The hooks used for corsets were considerably longer than those used on button shoes and spats. The long-handled hook was put through the loop - hooked the small round cloth-covered button, and *stressed* it into its loop – beginning at the larger-looser top and working down one button at a time until all two dozen of the buttons were fastened. "Hold it in Mollie, only a few more loops to go!" The story made the rounds about the bucksome lady, all gussied up nice and tight, sneezed and blew her buttons.

I never had any button shoes but my older sisters did. Those shoes came up above the ankle and also fit very snug. Papa and my older brothers all had spats which buttoned up around the ankles. They looked sharper than the later *zook-suit with the reet-plete.*

JUST FOOLING AROUND

I spent a lot of my time with a "n"-shooter. Back before the Civil Rights movement we were not troubled about using the "n" word. The n-shooters I made were not like the ones Great Grandpa used. He didn't have rubber bands such as the ones I had. The ones with which Grandpa used to shoot idle slaves was called a sling-shot – like King David used to kill Goliath. A slingshot consists of a couple of long leather thongs fastened to a pouch; non-the-less, that is where my shooter got its name. If Grandpa caught slaves leaning on their hoe or sitting on their cotton sack he would pop them with a pebble or a green cotton bole using his slingshot, hence the name.

One day I was shooting targets using green peanuts. My sister Pauline was the target. She was sitting on top of the barn, which was one of her favorite parking places. She would reach out and catch the peanuts and eat them. When I ran out of peanuts I found a small, hard, native pecan and without considering that it was a serious projectile I shot it accurately right in the middle of Pauline's fore-head. It almost unseated her and sure made her mad. She came down from her perch and came after me hell-bent for revenge. I hurriedly ducked out of sight around the barn and climbed up in the hay-loft and hid out behind some hay bales until I thought she had cooled off. She grew tired of searching for me and finally went into the house. I was sure that Mama had heard about my woeful deed and was preparing a severe sentence. I was praying she wouldn't tell Papa. He was a more severe disciplinarian than Mama.

While hiding out in the hay-loft I found a den with 4 baby kittens, their eyes were not yet open. I climbed down and ran to tell Mama about my discovery thinking that perhaps it might soften the penalty. Well—yes—but not much. I had to sit in the corner behind the cook-stove for a whole, long, long hour without food or water. The worse part was she confiscated my weapon.

The next morning, following my ordeal I could hardly wait to climb up into the hay-loft and see the baby kittens. I remembered where the den was, behind the hay bales and was disappointed when I discovered they were not there. Thinking that perhaps mama cat had hidden them someplace else it was time to do a search before telling Mama the bad news. I turned and saw this huge chicken-snake lying contentedly on top of the hay with four lumps down it's middle. Obviously, the four kittens had become lunch for a snake. That made me mad. I climbed down and found a sharp hoe, climbed back up and dealt severely with that mean old snake. The business end was the first to go. Without its head it was harmless. I dragged the old snake out to the wood-yard and chopped it in pieces between each lump. The little kitties were all dead. I still hate snakes.

UNCLE JOE MILLER

Uncle Joe is seated on the bottom right. My mother is on the top left.

My uncle Joe Miller was probably the funniest man I have ever known. He declared that he did not write the "Joe Miller Joke Book" but I still think he did, even though he had a very skimpy fifth grade education. He was always fabricating some funny gadget. For example, he had this hundred dollar bill, which he probably got in some poker game. He had cut some pages from a Sears catalogue the same size and shape as the bill, wrapped this hundred dollar bill around the outside of the rolled up stack so that it appeared like he had thousands of dollars. This was back in the hard-time days of the early twenties, when money was as scarce as hen's teeth so that when he would flash this huge roll of bills eyes would really pop. I suppose, like many, it was the first hundred dollar bill I had ever seen. I am not sure now, knowing Uncle Joe, whether it was real or phony.

Here is one of Uncle's favorite yarns: This cowboy, Rick Chambers and his old dog, named Dude had sat around cow-camps for so many years playing poker that old Dude had become proficient at the game. Rick and his old dog went into town one Saturday evening and went into the bar for a few and Rick got into a poker game with some other cow pokes. Rick had one beer too many and had to be excused. He turned his poker hand over to old Dude. When Rick returned and was standing looking over old Dude's shoulder. A Beer salesman happened to behold the unusual scene and remarked, "You mean that old dog can actually play poker?" Rick loosened his sweaty bandana, switched his tobacker to the other cheek and replied. "Yeh, but he ain't no good at it. Any body can beat him. You see, it's like this, when Dude gets a good hand he can't keep from wagging his tail."

Most every large family back in the early 1900s had at least one *black sheep* (an off-spring slightly south of what was considered to be the norm). Uncle Joe was a - less than desired off-spring, according to Grandpa Miller. Joseph's ambitions did not include farming, which might have been the reason for grandpa's less than cherished parent-child relationship. I do know one thing (according to Uncle Joe) he was famous for hiring on with Ringling Brothers Circus.

Whether or not he ever got further along with the circus than the poop-scoop and the tent-pin gang I can't be sure. His questionable achievements were in no small way believable. According to him he was a trapeze artist, a trick rider on the horses, a clown – which is likely. He was into some simple slight-of-hand tricks, like pulling a quarter out of my ear. His more famous trick was making a deck of cards disappear.

One of my memories of Uncle Joe was his old gray mare and his rickety, spring-seat buckboard. I remember well the time when he came home from somewhere after a long absence in his bouncy buckboard dragging an old T-model" ford chasse—with four flat tires, the deferential housing tied up with bailing wire, the engine block, gas-tank, radiator, plus a wash tub full of parts on the flat-bed of his buckboard. What on earth was he going to do with that rusty pile of junk? The three-door body was mostly absent. There was nothing but the frame, gas tank, wheels, motor, and much other stuff, but believe it or not Uncle Joe had a plan. He started with that pile of rusty junk and ended up with a motor-home that really worked, perhaps the first ever motor home. Here is one of my most amazing true stories about Uncle Joe Miller.

The very first thing Joe did with his pile of Model T junk was to clean, sand, and paint all surfaces to be painted. There was no such thing as sandpaper so he used just plain sand, the kind used in concrete aggregate. He piled it up and used axle grease, like that used to grease wagon wheels. The stiff grease gave the sand a clinging quality. He found an old, worn out cotton sack, salvaged some strips of ducking and tore them into about six inch strips like shoe-shine cloths and actually used them like shining shoes with the sand and grease to remove the rust and whatever. When everything was sanded thoroughly he took "drip gasoline," collected at oil well pump heads and washed the things clean and dry, then gave them a coat of black paint. When he finished with the pieces they looked even better than when they left the Ford Factory.

I am still amazed at Uncle Joe's method of redoing those "Model T" bearing surfaces. The crank-shaft and rod bearings were made with a soft metal called Babbitt – a mixture of copper, tin and anti-mony. Uncle Joe used old fruit-jar lids which are made from Babbitt. He used an old bullet-mold crucible to melt the jar-lids and bits of the old bearing surfaces down to a liquid. As I recall he found the main-shaft bearings sufficiently intact so that he could file away a thin layer of the bearing cap and the fit was sufficient. However the rod bearings all had to be completely resurfaced—caps and all. Uncle Joe made a mold of clay and squared up the shaft crank- throw in the molds and poured in the babbitt until it was over-filled and after they cooled down he would carefully file away the superfluous babbitt, down to the original castings. This would be necessary for each of the four rods and caps. Fantastic!

He then prepared a very sharp instrument to scrape away and square up the interior of the bearing, so that the fit was close but not tight. After carefully cleaning and greasing each of the bearings and tightening each cap he installed the huge old T-model flywheel with "V" magnets (part of the ancient ignition system) around the parameter, tightening it all up nice and tight. He could spin the fly-wheel and it would spin without binding anywhere. That was quite amazing. Obviously my uncle had an unusual talent for mechanics although he never pursued mechanical work after this that I know of. His two younger brothers Albert and Harry were very fine mechanics. Uncle Albert was more into machine operation than being a "Grease-monkey" according to Uncle Joe's folksy jargon. They both seemed to make a good life working on all kinds of automobiles here in Wichita Falls for many years. Uncle Albert had three sons and one daughter. Uncle Harry (Jack) had one son and two daughters. Their children all had an enviable opportunity to have a fine education.

I was so enamored by Uncle Joe's mechanical genius that I actually had to be coaxed away from the place. Mama sat in the buggy and called and waited and finally had to threaten me to get me away from Uncle Joe's fix-it operation. I spent the entire two mile journey home begging Mama to let me return the next day to watch Uncle Joe work on his Ford some more. She finally caved in and said yes. I didn't sleep well that night for thinking about all the fun Uncle Joe was having. He always seemed so contented when he was doing something he loved to do. If he wasn't whistling some strange tune of his own origin he was talking about his days in the circus. He never told me what his plans were or why he was so determined to get this rig finished and road ready. I suspect, from all accounts, Joe had the Montague County oil fields in mind. Obviously, he spent much time around Nocona, Caps Corner, Belcherville and St. Joe. Those were names of places he spoke of often. Another thing I know for sure was that he ended up married to a widowed lady who owned a large ranch just south of St. Joe. I visited him there when I was about 18 years of age.

After Uncle Joe finished re-constructing the old T-model, he found a slightly worn-out farm wagon bed, hardware and all with the covered-wagon wooden bows already fitted for the side-board pockets. All he had to do was cut out a hole for the gas-tank, fasten all four corners to the leaf-springs of the ford chassis, take the thing over to Alvord, buy a wagon-sheet, stretch it over the bows, tie it down and "bingo" he had a horseless, covered-wagon. It was the funniest looking thing you could imagine but it served Uncle Joe's need very well. He had a fold-up cot for sleeping, a kerosene camp stove with pots, pans, skillets, buckets, tin plates, cups for cooking and eating. He even had a special bucket for free casing-head-drip-gasoline for his Model-T engine. His living expenses were very minor and the oil-field pay was good. My dear uncle was in for the good life.

Finally, Uncle Joe Miller's covered wagon showed up in Belcherville, according to my old Nocona friend, Dick Walker, Sr. It seems my dear Uncle was the object of much curiosity when he sputtered into the old Belcher Pipe Yard one Monday evening. A crowd gathered around this strange rig as Joe pulled back on the steering wheel and yelled "Whoa," and climbed out. I am sure a large audience was a natural opportunity for him. According to Dick he went around to the front of his wagon-sheeted-rig and pretended to be unhitching a team of horses. Reaching out and patting each imaginary horse on the rump before reaching behind them to undo the tugs. The mouths of his audience must have opened even wider when he asked if he could water his horses there at the watering trough. He led them over to the trough and waited patiently for his imaginary horses to satisfy their thirst. Next, he slowly led them back over to his rig and tied them up. Uncle was a master at pantomime.

Joe then inquired as to whether there might be a job he could do to earn a little money. He was on his way to Oklahoma City, had to be there in a few days but had some time to help the folks there if he was needed. Yes, they needed a roust-a-bout on a spud-cable-rig over in the North Field. He could handle that. He hitched his imaginary horses back to his covered wagon, – lifted up on the crank, climbed into the driver's seat and went sputtering back down the road toward Nocona.

The huge steam rig was home to Uncle. He could slam the three foot crank pin home and apply his abundant weight, spin the huge flywheel, yank the steam valve open and get the thing going with the ease of any experienced grease monkey. He knew how to engage the idle pulley in its down position to tighten the drive belt, lift the cable tool to the drop auger and give the driller man as much speed as he demanded. I can just see Uncle Joe stretched out on the drawbar with the old drop-auger banging up-and-down "pow-pow-pow", and Uncle Joe's fallen chest muscles pulsing with the same rhythm "slosh-slosh-slosh." He learned to sleep lying in the bed of Grandpa's old farm wagon.

As luck would have it, the well came in the first night on the job. The heavy drop auger was reeled in and laid out for the swampier to clean, sharpened and make ready for the next well. It was necessary for the casing (large pipe) to be driven down to the oil sand to prevent a cave-in and then the crew, all but my dear uncle, left for the night. But Uncle, being ambitious for some fuel for his T model motor home, rigged an oval tin hood over the still gassing well, tied a stick to a crease in the tin hood, and set his beat-up gas bucket under the drip. Some of the cold Butadiene (heavy gas) striking the warm surface air condensed into a liquid, referred to as drip-gas. According to Walker, Uncle Joe found this beat-up, rusty, old oil barrel in a junk- pile. cleaned it up and in a few days had it full of free drip-gas and, as you might guess, he sold some of it for ten cents a gallon, to gather some change for his poker stash.

My dear old Uncle Joe had several tricks available, if needed, for his beloved poker game. One example, if he came up with a hand that was not profitable he had a trick leg that kicked the table over. His "old World War 1 battle injury" caused his leg to go crazy. (Joe hid out down on the King Ranch in South Texas until the war was over, according to Papa) He would get his card playing cronies "friendlied up" as he called it, to straighten his wounded leg before they could continue the game. While this was taking place, all the wrong cards could be righted and a winning hand practically assured. Another of his many tricks was to cut the cards in such a way that the game would have to be put on hold while the deck was being retrieved and reassembled. He could make the card deck disappear and re-appear at will. My dear old uncle was a true cardshark in every way known, at the time. He owned a small pistol, however it is doubtful that he ever used it. Uncle always seemed to be a kind and gentle person, at least on the surface and he did present a rather broad surface.

Uncle Joe must have spent several years around the North Texas Oil field. His vocabulary was thickly spotted with names like Belcher Ville, Ringgold, Nocona, Bulcher, Spanish Fort, Illinois Bend, Caps Corner and Saint Joe. He found his second wife south of Saint Joe, a widow who owned a rather sizable spread of ranch land (with oil). I once visited him there, back in 1923. I was into building crystal set radios about that time and always on the lookout for usable crystal materials. Prepared crystals could be purchased already imbedded in a round lead case for a dime, but I didn't have a dime. There was a thin layer of crystallized lead at the bottom of a deep gorge below Grandpa Miller's house that was very good but not very reliable.

Grandma Miller had a bunch of her in-laws and outlaws and their kids in for dinner one Saturday noon and I was explaining my radio fixings to Uncle Joe. He assured me that if I would come to his Saint Joe Ranch I would find a treasure trove of crystal in a deep cave not far from his ranch house. Any question as to how he knew so much about the geographic features of north Texas never entered my mind. He told me that if I would go over to the valley west of the school house and stay in that valley all the way north I would come to his house. The following Monday morning I decided to take a trip north on foot. It turned out to be a near thirty mile journey. I did as he suggested and sure enough, after a long half-a-day of fast walking it happened just as he told me.

I was walking along in a heavily wooded area—saw this dude sitting, leaning against a tree with his shotgun cradled in his arms. I went over to ask directions and sure enough it was my big fat uncle in person.

After his back-slapping "how'de" he asked me a dumb question, "Are ye hungry? Let's go up to the house and see if we can find something to eat." And, as usual he had to make a fun thing of it. He had me walk ahead of him to his house, which was not very far and as I was directed, Uncle Joe with his shotgun against my behind pushed me through the back door. He yelled at his wife to make me some lunch - saying I was "One of the bank robbers the sheriff was looking for, who had escaped from jail, over at the Montague County Courthouse." Aunt Jewel turned around and looked at me for a brief moment, started laughing and said, "Ah Joe, that's Dore's boy."

My dear old uncle spent the rest of the day showing me his gun collection and talking about his days with the circus. I spent a restless night, anxious for daylight to come so I could get out to that promised treasure-trove of crystals Joe had promised me. Aunt Jewel prepared me a very fine breakfast of hot biscuits, ham and eggs with grits, butter and molasses. I kept on wanting to talk about the cave but Uncle kept changing the subject. He was just too busy to take me to the cave. Perhaps if I came back some time later he might have more time. I should not have trusted my dear uncle's truthfulness and as a mater of fact, I never did again. There was no cave. My long walk was all for naught and I still had to walk all the way back home. My shoe-soles were already so thin I could step on a dime and tell if it was heads or tails. By the time I walked that near thirty miles back I was carefully watching out for grass burrs along the paths. "Thou shalt not bear false witness..." (Exodus 20:16) is a favorite Commandment along with *"Thou shalt not kill." (Exodus 20:13)* which I hope is not sinful if only the flash of a short, raging desire.

I likewise grew too busy after that to bother about hidden caves, crystals and radios. Uncle Joe Miller took his place along with the rest of my fading memories for some years. In the late 1930s my Uncle John Miller, the oldest of Oliver Miller's boys, moved Grandpa and Grandma Miller to Wichita Falls. Grandpa had suffered a severe stroke and Grandma was not able to care for him. Both of my Maternal Grandparents lived out their last days at Uncle John's house. They were interned back in the old Lake Valley cemetery beside the resting places of my Aunt Mille, Uncle Frank and another aunt whose name eludes my memory at the moment.

I am not aware of the details of the matter but I knew that Uncle Joe somehow ended up sick, and died at Uncle John Miller's house on York Street in Wichita Falls. I visited him there and remember vaguely our brief time together. It would have been after I entered the ministry. After having prayer with him before I left his bedside, I recall the last words he uttered to me as I was preparing to leave were, "It was fun while it lasted." He said it right after my prayer. Did he think my prayer was fun? It was a short prayer. No, in fact, I believe he was referring to his entire life. The greatest joys of his life seemed to be in making people laugh.

Actually Uncle Joe experienced one very sad periods during his life time. Beyond my memory, his first wife apparently had died quite young from a childbirth that went bad. My mother attended the funeral, wherever it was, and talked about Joe's wife, the mother in her casket with her baby in her arms. Joe could have been a very lonely man but he never allowed it to happen. He laughed and the world laughed with him.

A MYSTERY STORY

I have always liked mystery stories. I remember one such mystery story that involved my own doings. Pelly was a community about a mile east of my grandmother Harper's farm in Wise County, Texas. The Holiness Church there was having a revival meeting. I was never much inclined toward the Holiness Church and their holy doings but I liked their music. There was a guitar player playing for their revival that I considered to be the best of the best. His name was Fred Grimseley. Fred was a middle aged man at the time. He was a very out-going person and I loved to hear him play his guitar and sing.

It was on a Sunday evening that I saddled old Dick, my horse, and rode across-country to Pelly. I tied my horse to a nearby tree and went inside the church and found a seat, on the back row. Looking all around to see who was there that I would know and WOW! across the "crowded, room," I spied a stranger, a gorgeous teen age creature about my own teen age. She was tall, shapely, brunet, olive complexion, all the things I loved in my teen-age dream-girl. I learned, quickly, she was a niece of Fred Grimsley. Fred lived a mile or so north of Pelly. This beautiful little lady was his niece from Antlers, Oklahoma. Gee-Whiz! That was the longest church service in my memory. I can't recall what all might have happened during the service. I don't even remember Mr. Grimsleys music. Could I walk her home after church? Yes, that was permissible; holy-moley-doodel-dee

I untied my horse, and by her side, we began that thrilling journey to Uncle Fred's house. It was a lovely, half-moon night, almost too dark, but light enough to walk safely. I was holding her dainty, little hand in my right hand and leading old Dick, my horse with my left hand. Not exciting by today's courting standards but very interesting to me, then.

When we came to the old cemetery entrance across the road and down a ways north of the church house I saw a man standing behind a large cedar tree. It was Uncle Fred. I thought we left him back at the church house. We walked on. She was a great talker. Smart, too; she kept my mind solidly occupied with her conversation. She did not, for a minute allow my mind to wander. Further on we turned left on the road west and crossed Panther Creek, down and up the old wagon road. When we arrived on the other side, there stood Uncle Fred. He didn't pass us. How could he be there? O well—we continued our lovely journey. When we finally arrived at the Grimsley home, guess what? There, on the front porch, sat Uncle Fred. Do you suppose Fred Grimsley didn't trust me with his little niece or was he suffering from some kind of a guilt trip of his own?

GRANDMA'S TRIP TO TEXAS

My Grandfather, Joseph Harper, died in 1883 at the young age of 39. Papa was born in 1873, so he would have been 9 years old. My uncle Frank must have been about 13, Uncle William (Bud) about 12 and Uncle Moses was 8. My dear Grandmother, Bedy Jane Kierce Harper was terribly distraught; as the story came down to me. Her younger brother, Moses Kierce had migrated to Texas soon after the Civil War. He became like a surrogate father to my Grandmother Harper's four sons, his nephews. He taught them all about man things and some business dealings. He, himself, was very well established in the Texas town of Alvord as a cotton merchant and owned a hardware business there. When he heard about the death of his brother-in-law and the emotional condition of his sister he sent money for her and her four little boys to come to Texas. My Great Grandfather, William Harper hauled them down from north of Andalusia, along the Pee River to Mobile, Alabama by a wagon, drawn by a yoke of oxen. That would have taken at least four days (camping out at night). At Mobile they were ferried across the Yellow River and after many days layover were loaded onto a train bound for Texas.

Papa remembered very well the crossing of the Mississippi River at New Orleans, Louisiana. It had to be made by the old Civil War ferry. He recalled that the crossing took the better part of three days to complete. It was necessary that the ancient steam engine be hauled on board the large flat bottom boat and ferried across first and lined up on the rails. It was a long, tedious effort, hauling each of the coaches separately across with many interruptions. Some slow-downs were caused by paddle boat traffic on the river. Evidently there were many delays caused by break downs of their equipment. The huge ropes necessary to moor the ferry had to be hauled across the river by a steam powered paddle boat. Each of the seven or so coaches had to be taken across separately. After they were safely across and hooked up, the baggage was ferried across and then the passengers were transported onto the ferry and taken across.

According to Grandmother the train ride was not one of her cherished memories. There was a kind of enclosed privy at the end of one coach, which was nothing more than a hole in a bench - over a hole in the floor of the coach. The door would be locked when they came to a town. As they passed through some of the towns there would be people selling sandwiches and cookies. Grandmother didn't have much money to buy the food, so they were hungry most of the trip. I have no information as to the end of the rail line. I remember hearing

Papa talking about how they ended up traveling by stage coach. I am assuming that would have been the old Butterfield Stage Line that went west and north out of Dallas into Oklahoma. Papa said they were about a month making that long trip. Making that same trip today from Covington County, Alabama to Alvord, Texas by automobile would take less than two days.

Automobiles were becoming a common sight in Lake Valley in 1923. My Great Uncle, Moses Kierce (Uncle Mose, we called him) had a 1923 Model-T Ford. I was a nine year old restless dreamer. Some day I would own me a car, I mused.

Papa (left) and his youngest brother, Moses Harper, in front of a 1923 T-Model Ford (This T-Model belonged to my great uncle, Moses Kierce)

One Sunday afternoon Uncle Mose and Papa were going to Alvord for some reason or other. I begged Papa to let me go along.

He consented. They also took a woman Uncle Moses referred to as Aunt Thursa Miller (no relation); he jokingly called her "Aunt Friday," (More about her later) Since she was going, I would have to sit in the back seat with her. Well, Aunt Friday was about two axe-handles wide so that didn't leave mush room for me but I managed to squeeze in. I remember Uncle Mose telling her, "Aunt Friday you sit on the left side, I've got a bad tire on the right rear." That couldn't help much because she covered the whole back seat. Sure enough, before we got to Alvord he were rounding a left turn and "BANG" a blow-out on the right rear.

That was my first such experience and I hoped it would be my last. Uncle Mose had to unload Aunt Friday before he could jack up the wheel to fix it. Flat tires were as common as cockleburs back in those days. Mr. Firestone was learning how to make tires, but they sure must have had a long way to go. I learned, by experience, one had a flat about every time one made a trip. Jack up the flat tire, get out the tire-tools and pry off the old "Clincher-Rim" tire bead, pull out the inner tube, get out the "cold-patching" unscrew the lid which also had a rough side to "buff" the tube around the leak so the patch would stick. Then, take the bottle of cement, pull out the stopper which had a cotton applicator on a wire extended into the inside; smear the cement around the hole, then stick a lighted match to it and it would blaze up (for what reason I never knew. It worked just as well if you left the match off). then you cut a patch the size you needed and pealed off the layer of paper covering the sticky side of the patch and put it over the hole; then you rolled it hard to make it bond securely. Put the tube back into the tire, hang it on the rim, stick the valve stem through the hole in the wheel rim and apply the tire-tool. After you wrestled the tire back on you got out the hand pump and pumped air back into the tire; all fifty pounds of it. And, if it happened to be one of those hot Summer days in the Sun you used a lot of descriptive expletives, silently if ladies were present, otherwise, with lusty vigor.

Starting the motor on the old T could be a dangerous experience. There was much one needed to know that was written in the fine print. Some things to remember was to turn on the ignition switch, make sure the emergency brake was on, go around in front, take hold of the crank and if you remembered to position the spark lever up to a prescribed point, you spin the crank around until the engine started. If you forgot to adjust the spark lever up you might receive a broken arm or at least a sprained wrist. So, you learned, early on, not to forget to position the spark lever. If the engine was cold you had to *choke* it, meaning, to pull out on the wire with the loop protruding from the left lower corner of the radiator fastened to the carburetor that closed off the air intake butterfly valve forcing the vacuum from the manifold to draw gasoline into the firing chambers. If you choked it too much it would flood; get too much gasoline. The gasoline-air mixture had to be just right and sometimes that created rather large problems in starting the old T-model."

MOSES KIERCE SAGA

While driving from Sunset to Montague, Texas on FM 1749 a few years ago I saw a sign that read *"Pitman Holler Road."* The Pitman family, for whom the road was named, must have come from Virginia. Virginians have a strange way of ending about all words with the letter "R." The dictionary pronunciation would be "Hollow." The word "Hollow" means dry creekbed. If you go east on the road so indicated you would see why it was named "Hollow" or the Virginia version, "Holler." Papa often referred to it as "Dry Holler."

Pitman Holler was where my parents spent their honeymoon years. Apparently their first two children, Roy and Florence may have been born there. They later lived, for a short time in a place called Turkey Creek. Viven, their third child, could have been born there. Both of the locations would have had a Sunset, Texas address, but it's the Pitman Holler name that conjured up a most intriguing story. I heard Papa often talking about, his Uncle Moses Kierce living in a log-cabin at Pitman Holler. My Uncle Albert Miller, Mama's younger brother was one of the lead characters in the Moses Kierce saga and was my major source of information. Mama talked at length about some of the Pitman Holler episodes. The time was after the Civil War and near the year 1876.

My Great Uncle Moses Kierce, a young bachelor from Alabama, lived alone in a log-cabin at Pitman Holler. Early one cool spring morning he hitched his faithful team of steers to his old wooden beam mold-board plow to begin breaking ground for his crop. It must have been newly cleared land, because there was much brush and stumps to deal with. He had made one round and started another when he heard a baby crying. Surely it must be the wind blowing through the oak trees or a wild animal of some kind, he thought, so he moved on. However, on the next round, at the same location he again heard the same sound only this time much clearer. He stopped, the plow and went in the direction of the sound which seemed to come from some brush by a fallen tree. The downed tree had, what appeared to be, blood on one side of it. The soft sound of a baby crying was now well pronounced and he began to search franticly. His eyes then focused on a pile of leaves by the log and a tiny hand waving tremulously outside the leaf pile. Moses rushed over and picked the baby up from the leaf pile and discovered that the navel cord was still fastened to the placenta. He took out his pocket knife and carefully cut it loose. The little new-born infant was covered with ants. He brushed them off, took off his shirt and wrapped it around the skinny little body. He looked all around for the mother who had given birth to the tiny baby. She could not possibly be very far away. There was no one to be seen, so he carried it to his cabin to clean it up and see if he could find some way to feed it.

He had often seen his mother, Bedy Jane Kierce (my grandmother was the eldest of her two daughters and was also named Bedy Jane) create what she called a "sugar-tit" to pacify a hungry baby when its mother didn't have enough milk. He had churned a pat of butter only yesterday. All he would need more would be a spoonfull of sugar, a clean piece of cloth and a short length of string. It took only a few minutes to stir the sugar into the lump of butter, tie it up all nice and tight and form a little nipple for the tiny mouth to suck. First, he left the baby lying on his bed and pushed the pacifier into its face. Wow! The baby really went for the sugar- tit but as Moses watched, it seemed something was lacking. So he picked the baby up, sat down in his rocking chair, tucked the little baby snuggly in his big hairy arms and held the pacifier just so and began to rock and sing.

Soon the little baby was sleeping and he laid it tenderly on the bed. Returning to his rocking chair. he sat for a few moments watching the helpless baby sleep. Moses, stroking his long, heavy mustache, wondered—"what next?" Out of the corner of his eye, through the open door, he saw an Indian girl trying to get all of her skinny little body hidden behind an oak sapling in the front yard. She couldn't have been much more than fourteen years old. Obviously, she had something to do with that baby. Could it be that

173

she was the mother? Moses picked the baby up from the bed, carried it out front, laid it down on the grass, along with the remaining portion of the sugar-tit and moved back into the house out of sight. Then the shy little Indian girl rushed over, picked up the baby and disappeared into the thickly wooded area behind his cabin. Moses found his other shirt, put it on and returned to his team of oxen and plow. That would surely be the end of this outlandish experience, he mused. Actually, it was only the beginning of an episode that would shape the rest of his life.

The next morning Moses hitched his team of oxen to the breaking plow to complete plowing the land he had started the day before. When he came to the place where he found the baby he again heard a baby crying. Oddly enough this time it was lying on the same pile of leaves as yesterday, only it was now covered and he immediately recognized his old faded brown shirt. Stepping over the downed tree stump Moses picked the baby up. The dirty shirt was dirtier, smellier and wetter than it had ever been before. So he took off his clean shirt and again, wrapped it around the skinny little baby, shook some of the dirt off his old shirt and again headed for his cabin to do a clean-up job. He noticed for the first time that it was a girl and had an unusual amount of black hair. Another one of his sugar-tits was quickly created and shoved into the hungry little mouth. The crying ceased and all was once more peaceful. This time Moses laid the child on his bed and went about washing his shirt in soapy water, wringing it out as dry as he could, and put it on, knowing that the hot sun would eventually dry it out. He then turned back to his team of oxen and his rickety old plow. He glimpsed movement in the woods behind the cabin and was sure the mother would come back to his open cabin and take the baby away.

It was one of those hot steamy, North Texas days of early spring. Moses came in from the field as the sun was going down. He fed his yoke of oxen and his trusty saddle horse, threw some grain to the chickens and went in for a night of rest and refreshment. The little Indian lady and her baby would be long gone by now and it would all be only a fading memory. He drew water from his "dug well" and filled his wooden wash-tub with cool water; stripped off down to the bare and sat down—butt in—feet out for a refreshing bath. His nearest neighbor was at least three miles away and besides that his house was at the end of the trail. He was used to being the last house on the trail and had learned to like his brand of privacy. He sat there in his bath until the stars began to come out. When he was ready to get out of his bath he opened the stall gate and let his cattle and saddle horse drink the bath water. He went into his cabin, fried some salt-pork and potatoes and ate them with sourdough bread and buttermilk. After supper he took a quilt out of his trunk, spread it out on the grass in front of his cabin and lay there gazing up into the heavens until sleep came over him. The next thing he knew it was a new day. He busied himself attending to the morning chores, feeding his steers, Old Blue, his saddle horse, the chickens and milking old jersey, just like always. He wanted to ride into Forestburg. The

Butterfield stage was due to have run yesterday. There might be a letter from his folks back in Alabama.

His breakfast was ham, eggs and pancakes with steamy hot coffee creamed and sugared to taste. After he sat down and gave thanks and was ready for his first sip and bite he looked up and there stood little miss skinny holding a hungry baby with both fists crammed into it's little mouth, whimpering. For the first time in his entire life Moses lost his appetite. His breakfast became her breakfast and a sugar-tit was soon readied. Was he falling in love with a tiny, wet, dirty and hungry baby girl?

Moses Kierce was, for the first time in his life confronted with a problem he had no idea how to solve. He was a self-educated man who had learned to read, write, and cipher numbers and was a man with unusual manual and intellectual abilities. He had just recently signed a contract with a fabric company out of Dallas to do their cotton and wool buying. It would be next fall before that job would begin. He had been offered a position in Alvord working in a hardware business, which would serve him well with his cotton and wool buying contract. What on earth was he doing out here in the wildest, loneliest spot in North Texas creating sugar-tits and washing baby dirty out of his old shirt? God works in mysterious ways his wonders to perform. The answer to prayer often comes wrapped in strange, unexpected attire.

Moses later learned that the little Indian lady had been traveling with a family of marauding Indians. The Texas Rangers, threatening their safety, sent them hastily back across the Red River. This little lady's time of delivery came at a most inconvenient time and place. One of the older squaws must have stayed with her but was less than bold about showing up for the big white man with the handle-bar mustache. The new little papoose could have been her grand child, he thought.

Moses saddled old Blue for a trip over to Forestburg. His thoughts were all of that sweet, helpless little papoose. Where is she now and what could her fate possibly be, out in this wilderness of dangers? If she happened to survive the wilds of nature and reach adulthood would she be able to stem the tide of the dark pagan lore of her native world? Moses was the youngest son of a Christian Minister who also was a Master Mason. He was brought up in a secure Christian home with a devoted mother and a gentle but stern father, where the lures of evil were daily routed by prayers of Faith. So, every day of his bachelor life he would always began with a prayerful rededication to *"I am the way, and the truth, and the life:" (John 14:6)* The Holy Bible was his constant directive to faith and practice. He felt strongly urged that morning to make another one of his, now masterful, sugar-tits to leave in an obvious place for this tiny baby girl; just in case it might be needed before he could get back home.

It was a beautiful, clear, warm Saturday morning. Blue broke a sweat climbing up from the valley floor to the plateau above. The village of Forestburg seemed unusually quiet that Saturday morning. Moses was wondering if the stage had run yet. His answer was almost instantaneous. He saw a big cloud of dust approaching on the horizon from the south. That would be the old Butterfield clattering along the rough, un-graded road-way. Moses dismounted, untied the feed-bag from behind the saddle and hung the strap over old Blue's head which immediately dropped it to the ground and began munching on his lunch of oats. Moses dropped the bridle reins over the hitching rail and went into the Brady Racket Store to buy a small bag of sugar, a sack of 45 cartridges, a cake of soap and some candy sticks. He was still thinking about the little Indian lady and her papoose. The little squaw might like some sweets to help shape her skinny little body into a more attractive profile and also provide enough breast milk to feed her little papoose.

In the meanwhile, the Butterfield Stage came to a grinding stop in front of the old log depot across the road. The three-team hitch was being loosed from the stage coach and driven over to the wagon-yard where a fresh team was being harnessed and readied for the next leg of the journey; which would be Red River Crossing. That is where the Butter-field had standing reservations for the night. Only one of the six passengers was getting off at the *Burg*. The others got out to stretch, have coffee, cookies and what ever relief that was necessary. There was that usual line of ladies waiting in front of the out-house privy. It had been converted into a three-holer but the ladies always went in only one at a time. The men folks all gathered over behind the wagon yard for an informal relief and the usual chit-chat, along with the drovers and horse wranglers. The shot-gun man (armed guard) tossed the mail-bag down, climbed down from his seat, leaned his shotgun against a rear wheel of the stage coach and took a hefty chew of tobacco. He was not permitted to chew when the stage was in motion. Tobacco spitting into the wind was not good for business.

The mailbag was carried inside, opened and the mail sorted. There was no letter from Alabama. Moses had one other thing to do. He had brought a couple of plow sweeps over to the black-smith shop last Saturday to have them sharpened; he would not need them for two or three weeks but he should pick them up because he had planned on going to Alvord next Saturday. He had some business there that needed his attention.

So, slapping old Blue fondly on his big broad rump, to get his attention, Moses reached in and tightened the flank girt, taking up two holes in the cinch strap, folded the feed-bag and tied it behind the saddle. He placed his grocery purchase in one saddle-bag and the sweeps in the other, picked up his reins, swung him-self lightly into the saddle and galloped off in the direction of Pitman Holler. By the time he came to the valley floor the evening shadows had begun to lengthen and a cool south breeze caused him to push his old hat back. Patting old Blue, for a slower pace he began to sing. "What a Friend We Have in Jesus all our sins and grief's to bear, what a privilege to carry every-thing to God in prayer." Moses then raised his voice in an audible prayer, lifting his hand as if to touch the hand of God.

"Home sweet home, be it ever so humble there's no place like home." That was the urge for the last few hundred yards before home.

It was old Blue's arrival theme as well. He speeded up to an easy short-lope eagerly pushing on the reigns. He always knew that a stop in front of the cottage was par for the unloading process and also that his master dismounted and mounted from the left side. So he stopped with his left side in front of the cabin door. Moses dismounted, loosed the two straps to his saddle-bag, took out his groceries and went into the kitchen-dinning area to store his purchase. He turned to take old Blue out to the barn and noticed his old shirt on the bed all crumpled up. But wait, there was something underneath it.

Moses reached over to pick up his old dirty shirt and discovered little papoose lying there, as still as death, with the whites of its eyes exposed. He quickly picked the baby up, held it to his ear listening for a heart-beat. There was indeed a very faint pulse. He then grabbed a pillow and emptied the case, wrapping it around the baby, ran out the door and swung into the saddle holding the lifeless baby in his right arm. Old Blue seemed to know that this was an emergency. He whirled around and headed back toward the *Burg* full out.

Doctor Wright was out on a call. He was also the local horse doctor but his wife, according to some of the town's folks was a better doctor than her husband. She took little papoose in her arms, turned it on its tummy and it let out weak cry. She looked over at Moses and said, "This baby is starving and terribly dehydrated. We have to do some-thing quickly or it will die." She found a syringe, filled it with water and forced a few drops into the tiny mouth. After waiting a few seconds she again forced some drops of water between the tiny blue lips. The baby coughed slightly and swallowed. Elsie Wright looked up at Moses and smiled. "That is a good sign. She must be a tough little Indian. Where in the world did you find her?" Moses wiped a stream of tears from his bearded face on his sleeve and began to unfold his story.

By this time Dr. Wright rode up, noticed Moses' horse in front of his house and went in to make sure his visit was legitimate. He quickly surveyed the scene and offered his prognosis—"That kid is jist hongry. You need to feed it. Where in hell did you ever come up with an Indian kid, anyway?" Elsie, ignoring her rough-shod husband went into the kitchen and came out with a tumbler of milk and a small pitcher of honey. She very methodically measured out a small amount of milk and added a few drops of honey, stirred the mixture thoroughly, lit a kerosene lamp, held the mixture over the flame for a moment and then again, used the syringe to feed it drop by drop into a hungry little mouth. After a few minutes of being fed, little papoose seemed to be coming around satisfactorily. Elsie turned to Moses and recommended that he should leave the baby with her until tomorrow. There were other things she could do to make life better for baby.

The trail that wound its way back down to Pitmanholler seemed much longer than usual. Moses reined old Blue back to a slower pace. It was necessary that he have time to talk to the Lord about this most tender situation confronting him. All shapes of what-ifs moved through his mind but were soon refreshed with a calm that seemed to surround him like the cool fragrance of the valley.

As Moses passed by the open front door of his cabin he saw what appeared to be the little Indian mother lying face down on his bed with her face buried into his old dirty shirt, likely believing her little papoose to be dead. He had in mind a plan for sharing the good news that papoose was not dead but alive and well.

After slowly dismounting he led old Blue on down to the barn, undid the saddle cinch, lifting the saddle and blanket off together, taking the bridle off with his free hand and hanging them on their special rack. He filled the feed trough with a good size helping of oats for old Blue and stopped by the well to drew several buckets of water and emptied them into the watering trough. The moment had come: How was he going to announce his good news to a grieving mother who could not understand English?

Moses moved through the cabin door with an air of ***all is well***. He was, not only aware of the little lady lying face-down on his bed but there was an older squaw also in the room, sitting in the corner on the floor across from the head of the bed. Moses sat down in his creaky old rocking chair at the foot of the bed, crossed his legs, stroked his long mustache and spoke assuriengly: "May the good Lord Bless and keep you." The skinny little mother quickly got up from the bed, apparently afraid for a moment. Her eyes were red from weeping. Holding the dirty old brown shirt tightly to her breast it was obvious she considered her baby to be dead. The question she had, was acted out by pretending to be digging in the ground: "where did you bury my baby?" Moses stood, slowly, smiling, understanding her question and answering slowly in English: "Your baby is alive and well." At that moment the older squaw stood, moved over to her and spoke some words in their native language. She must have understood. The little mother's eyes brightened, now filled with tears of joy. Her next question was anticipated "Where is she?" Moses turned to the older squaw who apparently understand some English and said: "I left little papoose with the medicine man (doctor) over at Forestburg. The medicine man wanted to give her some more special food to help her get well. She is going to be just fine. I will go in the morning and bring her to you." The older squaw translated the information to the little mother who than ran over to Moses and knelt down as if in worship. Moses reached down, picked up her quivering little body and held it close to his. Her joys were now immeasurable. She laughed and wept uncontrollably.

Moses Kierce realized that for this delicate little papoose to survive it was going to be necessary for him to take control of her and bring her living conditions up to the 19th century. A primitive life with the Comanche Indians would likely end in the baby's death. Moses would have to make room for the three of them in his small cabin. It would be necessary for the older squaw to remain in the mix. His being a bachelor would raise a lot of eye-brows. He would need to clear the idea with the older squaw and if she was in agreement he would add another room to the old log cabin.

He arranged with the squaw for her and the young mother to spend the night in his cabin and he would stay the night in the boarding house over in Forestburg. He had promised the good people at the Baptist Church he would bring the Sunday morning Bible message and that would give him more time for preparation. The permanent housing arrangement could be brought up later.

Moses went out into the garden and found a good sized cabbage head, four medium sized turnips and some green onions. He brought them into the kitchen, built a fire in the cook stove and put a teakettle of water on to heat. The cabbage had to be diced and the turnips sliced. The older squaw stood up and offered to assist him. She took his butcher knife and began as though she was familiar with the chore. Moses set the bacon grease out and pointed out the other necessary ingredients for the vegetable dishes.

He then went into the cow barn, brought out a half-bushel of cotton-seed to feed old Jersey. Jersey's big heifer calf was anxious to do her chore by nursing and punching the udder for mama to give her milk down. After her greedy act, a rope was clipped onto her halter and tied off until the milking was finished. While old Jersey munched on her supper, Moses sat down on his old three-legged milking stool on her right side, placed the two gallon bucket on the ground under her udder and proceeded to milk out three of her four teats. He used both hands, milking two teats at a time. In five minutes he would have a gallon of good rich, fresh milk. He then turned the calf loose to finish its supper.

Moses moved quickly back to the kitchen, strained the milk through a cloth into a crock-jar and set it aside in his water cooler. Grits was a specialty for the Kierce family. Moses always made enough at breakfast to have leftover fixings for some corn-pone. He chopped the green tops from the onions, cut them up fine and mixed them into the grits mixture, poured the contents into a hot skillet, turned it over and over until it browned well on both sides. Then he brought out one of his jars of pork sausages (packed in lard), opened it and placed the contents into the skillet to heat. In the meanwhile the cabbage and turnips, prepared by the older squaw were ready to dish up. The drink was coffee or grape wine. The plates and flatware were already in place. Moses was now so looking forward to sitting down at the table with his make-believe family.

The little Indian mother began to reach for the corn-pone. Moses took hold of her hand, bowed his head and gave thanks, then began to help her plate to a large wedge of the corn-pone, a sausage and some of the vegetables. It was obvious the little mother had no ideas about Moses' family protocol. The older woman seemingly was embarrassed about the lack of manners exhibited by her young companion. It was becoming more and more obvious to Moses that the little mother was not accustomed to the ways of white English speaking people. She would need instructions on how to eat with a knife, fork and spoon. But before he could think about teaching her the older squaw took over.

Sitting around the table after supper felt wonderful to Moses. All of them were so relaxed that conversation came natural. Moses had a lot of questions, "Who are these two women? Where did they come from, to which Indian tribe do they belong and why are they still hanging out around the holler?" Soon Moses would know the answers to these questions. The older lady was first to identify herself. Her name was Thursa, the young mother was her half brother's daughter and her name was Roxie. The father of little Jeanie, that was the baby's name, had been killed by Texas Rangers only a few days ago. There was considerable fighting along the Red River in the 1880s. Quanah Parker and his scouts were determined to hold the territory south of the river. Texas Rangers along with the Militia were kept busy keeping the Comanche across the river.

Thursa's Sister, Carrie, had married a man named Dave Cantrell. Dave's parents owned the 160 acre farm adjoining my Grandfather Oliver Miller's farm on the south. Uncle Moses Kierce helped my Grandmother, Bedy Jane Harper, buy half of that Cantrell land. But I am getting ahead of my story. Thursa happened to be dating a good friend of Moses, named John Miller (No kin to my grandfather). John had been working at a ferry crossing on the Red River, at a place called Illinois Bend. Roxie's parents usually spent their summer months across the river in the Oklahoma territory. Thursa had been working as a maid for the Haralson family. That was the way she had become fairly affluent in the English language and customs. John and Thursa planned on being married. Moses knew John to be a fine Christian man.

How come Thursa to be in Pitmanholler? It seems the Comanche Chief asked her to go back and stay with Roxie until she was able to finish her trip, since she was familiar with the area. The two women and the baby had been sleeping in a bed of leaves in the wooded area behind Moses' cabin as they waited until Roxie gained enough strength for the journey back to the territory. They had been surviving by their Comanche skills, knowing what is edible, and how to find and prepare it. Thursa had managed to trap a young fat rabbit in a briar thicket and found an abundance of "lambs-quarter" and "poke-salad" greens, things they could eat raw. They did cook the rabbit pieces on a stick over a campfire. However, there was nothing for little Jeanie except to nurse, and Roxie had little if any milk. Moses soon learned that the sugar-tits he created for the baby had been consumed mostly by the little mother.

After washing the dishes, putting things away and with the help of Thursa the bedding arrangements were discussed and made ready. Moses saddled old Blue and headed for Forestburg. It would be late when he arrived but he felt sure Elsie Wright, who also owned and ran the only boarding house his side of Montague, would have room for him. Moses arrived slightly after sunset and found Dr. and Mrs. Wright sitting on the veranda. Yes, they had a vacancy on the second floor. Moses rode old Blue over to the wagon yard, unsaddled him and took his saddle, blanket and bridle into the tack room and placed them on the rack which only had two other saddles, saw that old Blue was properly fed and watered. He then went back to the tack room, took his Bible and dress-up clothes out of his saddle-bag and walked back to the rooming house.

Little Jeanie was awake with her thumb and a finger or two in her mouth. Her little legs were kicking vigorously. Moses had never beheld such a lovely little creature. She was dressed in a pink diaper, pink night shirt and even a little pink bow in her black hair. It was impossible for him not to take her in his arms. He had never felt a love like this in his life. It was a feeling that could never go away. But how on earth could he possibly continue this relationship?

Moses sat down in a rocking chair, holding little Jeanie close to his breast. He began to rock and croon. "Little baby sweet and fair; God who's love is everywhere. Bless this little one we love with endless blessings from above." Soon little Jeanie was asleep but he could not bring himself to put her down in her rocking bed. Elsie, overcome by the fatherly scene, wiping her eyes, went back out on the veranda. Moses sat for a long time holding little Jeanie, silently praying, "Dear Lord how can I make this bond of pure love last for the rest of my life?" Finally he put the baby back in her cradle, said his good nights to the Wrights, picked up his Bible and bag and went up to his bed room.

Moses opened his bible to First Corinthians chapter 13: That seemed to be the right place to began his sermon preparation. "Though I speak in tongues of men and of angels but have not love

I am nothing;" But what if I have love?—"I have everything necessary for the good life." The next point would naturally be: "Love does not come with a cheap price tag." The final point to make is—"Love lasts forever." The summary would be: God is love and if we have that connection-"Nothing shall ever separate us from Love." The sermon title would be "THE LOVE CONNECTION." Moses went to bed and slept soundly until the morning sunlight bathed his face in its glory. According to his big old Ingersoll pocket watch; it was 7:45—almost time for the Breakfast Call. He hurriedly got dressed and made his way down to the dining room. Shaving and dressing for church would have to wait until later.

There were only five people at the long breakfast table that Sunday morning. Ned Potter and his wife Nellie, were the only ones Moses knew. The other three were cowboys on their way back to Fort Worth after the long cattle drive to the rail head in Kansas. Ned was the local ice man. He had removed the back seat of his surrey and fastened the heavy icebox in its place. He provided ice to the drugstore and sold ice to who ever would need it. He had to haul it from the icehouse in Alvord. After speaking to Ned and his wife and acknowledging the other three; Moses signaled for a time of silence for his usual lengthy invocation.

After a delicious breakfast of two eggs over easy, a thick slice of ham and four or five fluffy biscuits with sweet cream butter oozing out over the wild plum jelly, cups of hot coffee Moses was ready for whatever might lie ahead. He returned to his room to shave and finish his preparation for the morning service.

Moses was warmly greeted that Sunday morning, especially by the ladies of the church. The men only shook his hands and grunted their approval. He couldn't escape the giggles, coy glances and quiet verbal expressions by the younger boys "way-to-go Mo". However by the time Moses stepped into the pulpit the mood become more somber. He explained, first of all, how by keeping our minds open to the guidance of the Holy Spirit the many facets of the abundant life are always ready to open to us. "This unexpected, magnificent caption for my entire future has unfolded before me. For me, I have always known, It is no secret what God can do."

After Moses said amen and the parting hymn was sung, he headed for Irene Wright's dining room. The usual Sunday noon crowd was present and waiting. The, baby, Jeanie, was the center of attention. All the ladies had to hold her and coo. Moses was as proud as any father could be. Irene had dressed her in a long white dress with pink ruffles and pink crocheted bootees. Jeanie was a beautiful baby.

After dinner was finished Irene took Moses aside to show him how to feed little Jeanie. Irene had found a small drinking glass that could be used with much caution. She filled it with milk, warmed and stirred in a spoon-full of honey. She had Moses sit down and hold Jeanie as upright as possible and hold the glass against her lips and introduce a tiny bit of milk in-between her lips, until she began to ingest it and then very slowly as not to over do and cause her to strangle. Moses soon got the hang of it and sat lovingly feeding his little one. "You have a good milk-cow but do you have any honey?" Irene inquired. "No I do not have any honey, however if you can spare a little to tide me over for a few days I will be going to Alvord. They will have some there." Moses said as he began to pack things in for his home-ward move. "I will prepare a small jar that will last you for the week," Replied Irene. While Irene finished collecting the clothes and honey Moses walked over to the wagon-yard to hitch old Blue to a buggy which was leased for the occasion. The buggy was fairly new and very clean and shiny. Moses thought to himself, "I'll need to buy one of these first time I am in Alvord. If I am to be a family man....Um, 'hope springs eternal.'" He loaded his saddle and bridle in the back and drove over to the boarding house to load up his most precious cargo to go home.

This home-coming was an event of great joy. The mother, Roxie and aunt, Thursa took turns holding and loving baby Jeanie. They had never seen a baby dressed in such finery. Mother Roxie had much to learn about feeding and tending to her little one. Aunt Thursa was a special presence to help Moses with his next days ahead. It was possible for her to spend some time with them. She was a great teacher for Roxie. Both women and baby Jeanie would live in his log cabin and he would sleep out in the barn until he could make better arrangements.

Moses had about finished his spring plowing. June corn could be planted in a few days. About 10 acres would do for the June corn. He had planned to plant 15 acres of cotton. That would be his only money crop. It would be a while before the ground would be warm enough for planting cotton. In the meantime he could ride over to the county seat and have a chat with the county judge about his concern for little Jeanie. Would it be a likely thing to marry mother Roxie? Could he adopt baby Jeanie? What would he need to do to arrange for these things to happen? He had already talked to Aunt Thursa. The only thing she knew was that Moses would need to contact Chief Quanah Parker and purchase the right for such an arrangement.

Moses packed a lunch for himself and filled old Blue's feed bag with oats. Then saddled old Blue and headed for Montague. It would take half the day, Monday, to cover that distance. He arrived in the afternoon and fortunately the Judge was not busy. Judge Bob Faulkner warmly welcomed Moses into his office seated him and offered him a cup of coffee, which Moses accepted. The Judge opened the conversation with the usual, "What can I do for you?" Moses already knew and unloaded his burden of questions. Faulkner had to think a long time in silence. He then stood up, turned to his library and selected two books. He turned to the index in the larger of the two books, moistened his thumb and forefinger and checked the index and began flipping through the pages until he found his place. Two "grunts" and one "hum" later he began answering questions. "There ain't no law agin your marrien a squaw, iffin that's what'che wont. Gist give me a minute to look at what the Comanche laws book has to say, if anything." Again Judge went through the finger moistening routine. "Guess what old feather-bonnet would settle for? He would settle for one young buffalo and two chickens." Where would Moses most likely find the Chief? Not much telling. Most likely up around Illinois Bend; that is where he spends the summer - sometimes. The other night, some of his scouts stole a big black stallion from Oliver Miller (my grandfather). That is where the tracks crossed the Red River so he probably is still there somewhere. "If you see Miller's stud horse over thor let me know. I'll haf-ta try and get im back. Oliver is pretty upset about it. He wanted to go after them thievin redskins but I managed to talk him out of it. He'd gist git his self killed. And you better take care. Old feather-bonnet can git awful upset."

Moses headed back to Pitmanholler. He now knew what he would have to do. As he came to the trail that turned off to Pitmanholler he met, of all people, John Miller. John was Thursa's intended, so he would be the right person to help him complete his plans. John was working at the river crossing at Illinois Bend and would be the one who would know the in's and out's about where to find Chief Quanah Parker and making the trade for his bride to be and baby Jeanie. John Miller turned aside and spent the night with Moses. John was happy to see Thursa. They were to be married soon.

Moses' marriage plans must be made. Why could he and Roxie not be married the same time as John and Thursa? That would simplify things for both couples. Moses had not yet asked Roxie if she would be his wife. He would need to do that through an interpreter.

So he asked Aunt Thursa to pop the question for him. She did and Roxie's face lit-up with an ear-to-ear smile. She ran into his waiting arms as if to give herself to him in total. Moses always referred to it as a left-handed proposal. The date set to be married was the same time John Miller and Thursa had planned. John followed Moses out to his bedding place in the barn. Their conversation quickly turned to Moses' housing need. Would he add on to his old log cabin or build a proper house elsewhere?

John Miller knew where he was to live. His father-in-law owned 160 acres of land on which he had built a large house in the Lake Valley Community. Thursa had to share it with her sister, Carrey who was married to Dave Cantrell. Dave had built a very fine home on his wife's 80 acre half.

John knew of a fine place in the Pleasant Hill Community. It belonged to the late Celesta Carmonadi. He had recently passed away and his only son, a business man in Dallas had it up for sale, household furnishings, all farm equipment and animals. That would be a really good purchase for Moses. Moses could get in touch with him through Edwin Pinnilunni. Ed, who lived close by, had been a good friend of the Carmonadi family. The Pinnilunni, Carmonadi, and Fenoglio families all migrated from Italy in the late 1700s. Celestial had requested that Ed take charge and tend to the farm and find a buyer. His wife had died a year or so earlier. They had only the one son. Moses and John would ride over in the morning to look it over.

Tuesday morning began with the sun peeping through the post-oak trees and old Jersey bellowing for her big heifer calf and some one to milk her and feed her. Moses went about tending his morning chores as usual, followed by John Miller. Thursa had prepared breakfast of coffee, hot griddle-cakes with fresh churned butter and sorghum molasses. Moses was especially thankful that morning. His Thanksgiving prayer lasted for at least 10 minutes; he later admitted.

What would Moses need to do to adopt little Jeanie, marry Roxie? Big Chief Quanah Parker would expect his dowry. John Miller would know. Surely he had been in touch with the Chief, if his marriage plans were complete to marry Thursa. No, John had not been to see the Chief. Thursa had given him instructions on how and where he could get his pre-nups all in order according to Comanche customs. Moses had already investigated the Texas requirements and received questionable council from Judge Faulkner concerning Indian requirements. He and John Miller would have to join their information about their nuptials status and go together to confront the Chief of the Comanches.

Celestial Carmonadi, like most of the Italians who settled around Montague County were great wine connoisseurs. He left a large wine-grape vineyard along with a sizeable fruit orchard. What Moses didn't know was that not only did he leave a great barn and a somewhat great house but also a deep wine cellar with a stock of fine wine. Since Moses was a teetotaler, according to His Baptist Discipline, his first reaction was to destroy it; pour it all out. But,

Edwin Pinnilunni assured him that the Italian Community would pay him a handsome price for his Carmonadi Wine. He would speak to the Catholic Priest over at Saint Jo. Sure enough it was needed. The Carmonadi brand was already known and welcomed by the mostly Italian church membership. Moses must have received a handsome price. He had no idea what kind of a price to ask for, but that was not necessary. The Carmonadi name alone, would bring the price up to a welcoming height for Moses.

Lake Valley was a little known community south-east of Montague. As a matter of truth it wasn't mentioned in the Fenoglio History book. The name somehow escaped everybody but the tax collector. It was originally located on the north banks of a rather sizable lake of some note, hence the name Lake Valley. Some years latter Grapevine Creak washed into and drained the lake. The dry lake bed depleted much of the village surrounding the north west end of the lake. I can recall the blacksmith shop, a grocery store and the junky remains of an old steam powered cotton gin there.

One of the early settlers was a government surveyor named Lonny Burros. According to some historic scuttlebutt Lonny was a homely, scraggily bewhiskered little guy who walked with a limp, one leg shorter than the other. He had surveyed for himself a choice 160 acre farm near the lake valley school survey. The only young ladies he seemed to be able to attract were some of the little Indian teens from across the Red River from his grandmother's place near Spanish Fort. According to one source he married one of the little

Comanche girls, and built a good house on the north end of his 160-acre survey. There are no actual records but it seems he fathered two half-breed daughters, Thursa and Carrey. Thursa married John Miller and Carrey married Dave Cantrell.

John and Thursa Miller had seven children, three girls and four boys. John was a voice to be listened to in the Valley. He was president of the school board. The Lake Valley school was a small two teacher school but had a complete high school. Although John himself had very little education and Thursa even less, they were determined that their children would finish high school. [Baptismal picture Miller tank]

John Miller's stock tank with Papa at the end of the line assisting in the baptism.

The Millers were faithful members of the Baptist Church. They lived only a few hundred yards east of the church house, so it was convenient for him and his family to be custodial church members. They had a large stock pond about a hundred yards east of the horse barn. That pond became the place for all of the baptismal services for the church. In later years the telephone switchboard was located at their house. Their daughter Nancy, was a Sunday school teacher and the switchboard operator. The John Miller home was the center of the social activities of the Valley. Not many weeks passed that they did not have a community singsong, a fiddle band gathering, with ice cream and cake. The whole family loved to eat. Thursa and two of her daughters became a bit over weight.

Mose Kierce, Roxie and Jeanie

I LEFT THE FARM

One hot, summer day in July of the year 1932; My life was to change forever. I was plowing the south corn field with a walk-behind cultivator powered by a team of mules. My head was throbbing with a dry-sinus headache. The dust and heat was unbearable. I plowed until noon then unhitched the team and went to the house. It was lunch time. I managed to feed the mules and by the time I reached the house I was too sick to eat lunch. My mother gave me some pain medication (aspirins) and I went out on the back screened-in porch where there was a bed. I lay down for a considerable time and finally was relieved enough to fall into an exhausted sleep. At one o'clock sharp, my father called out to me that it was time for me to get back to the plowing chore. I sat up in bed and immediately had to lie back down. My throbbing sinus headache was back with a vengeance. My father came back a second time and proceeded to scold me severely. I tried once more but couldn't do it. I was about to tell my father what I thought about him and his damned farm when he appeared a third time. This time he picked up an old cane-bottomed chair and threatened to strike me with it.

I got up and went to the barn as if I were going to work, but I kept on going until I came to the rail-road water tank where a freight train was taking on water (days of the old steam-trains). This was about two miles away from home. There I found a safe place to ride and rattled on west to Wichita Falls. I went to my sister Flaura's house and collapsed, sick and exhausted. I suppose my sister wrote my mother telling her where I ended up because sometime later my mother bundled up what few clothes I had and sent them to my sister. Where could she have found that much money for the postage? I was attempting to completely separate myself from my father.

Times were desperate after the Stock Market crashed. I wore the soles out on my shoes looking for work. There was a shoe shop over on Van Buren Street that needed business but had to have money to operate. I needed to have my shoes resoled but was broke. No money. The shoe cobbler had a stack of circulars he wanted distributed and he would resole my shoes if I would distribute his circulars. But would he do the resoles first? My cardboard innersoles were worn down to the stockings again which also had holes. He was a kind man and would; so I removed my shoes and waited.

An hour or so later I had new soles on my shoes. I was handed 1000 circulars and instructed to put one in every door for all the blocks surrounding the shoe shop and beyond until I ran out. Putting out 1000 circulars, one in every door required a lot of walking. By the time I had finished, my new soles were worn so thin I could step on a dime and tell if it was heads or tails. Maybe they would last until I could do better.

What to do? I could join the WPA, one of President Roosevelt's fix-it remedies for the Great Depression, but that was not my ticket. Back out on the streets again; surely anything would be better than sleeping in a box and going hungry. Then it was I landed a job with Morris Blank's fruit stand on the corner of Holliday and Eleventh street, as night watchman for one dollar a night. Not much, but it beat chopping fire wood with a dull ax for fifty cents a rick. That job lasted for about six weeks. I was cleaning the place up on that final morning, getting ready for the day's run when I picked up one grape that had fallen to the dirt floor, brushed the dirt off against my dirty trousers and ate it. Well now, my dear old Jew boss, Morris Blank, was peeping around the corner and beheld one of his precious grapes being consumed by, of all things, his hired hand, this country bumpkin from the Valley and so I was immediately fired.

I took my one dollar salary for the night and strode sadly away. That would have been during the hot Summer of 1932, not a very good year. I walked down town to the produce market along the railroad tracks where another brilliant business man gave me another fantastic job. I was given a sack of old Irish potatoes a gunny-sack and a bucket of water. I was to soak the old potatoes in the water and rub the skins with the gunny sack until they resembled and could be sold as "new potatoes." Needless to say this country kid couldn't contribute his talents to such chicanery in good conscience. So, I was walking the streets once more looking for a job.

As a child growing up I learned a good lesson - *pull your own weight*. I never missed any meals as a child at home but I was reminded many times that I must earn my own bread by the sweat of my own brow. Papa and Mama never accepted handouts from anyone. That became a part of my own résumé for life.

MY LEAP OF FAITH

He ere I am relating a series of miracles that I did not understand. I yet look back with a sense of awe. How could a country bumpkin from a poor Wise County farm, with a very inept eighth grade education ever end up married to a noted Pipe Organist, earn a BA degree from an elite university like Texas Christian University, complete a sufficient amount of seminary studies to receive Ordination into Christian Ministry? This is a story too big to tell but I will try.

The story begins in 1936. I was hitch-hicking from Amarillo, Texas to Wichita Falls when a model A ford coupe stopped and a voice from within called out, "Can you fix flats?" My answer was yes so I was invited to come aboard. The voice belonged to Walter Freiberg, a man destined to become my cousin by marriage. Walter Freiberg was a young attorney trying to make his way. He was coming from New Mexico where he had been sent to repossess the model A Ford. The tires were badly worn and Walter was not anxious to be fixing a flat tire on that hot summer day. That is how I first became acquainted with Walter Freiberg.

I was living with my older sister, Mrs Flaura Magness in North Wichita Falls at that time. Living at the Harper farm, as I have explained, was history. I had not had the good fortune of being able to complete high school. I was keenly aware that if I ever hoped to reach the summit of any future goal in life it would be necessary to, somehow, finish my education. How am I to do that?

My cousin Harold Miller of Wichita Falls had just completed a four year tour of duty with the United States Navy and in the process had ended up with a pretty good education. Perhaps that would be my best opportunity. Next morning I visited my older brother, Roy Harper who had a watch shop at the corner of Ninth and Scott, Streets. I tried to talk to him about my renewed hope. He was rather un-committing. I set out to go to the Navy Recruiting Station over on Ohio Street with the intension of joining the Navy. A block north on Scott Street I was curious about some goings on at the Sears Roebuck store on the corner of Tenth and Scott. They were adding a ready-to-wear department. There must have been over a hundred men and women standing in a line that ended at the Sears office, applying for work. The great depression was still much with us and work was most impossible to come by. I recognized a young man about my own age whom I had met somewhere, putting some clothes-racks together in the new addition of the store. He was having consider-able difficulty in getting the right part in the right place so I stopped and offered my assistance. The construction was completed and I was discussing my Navy plan with him. A short, dapper gentleman, immaculately dressed, came up to us. As it turned out he was a Mr. Helms, who at that time was vice president of Sears Roebuck and Company, with an office in Chicago. He told the young man with whom I was visiting, (sorry I do not recall his name) to go clean up behind the carpenters who were working the building. Then he turned and asked me to go up to the third floor and start putting some furniture together. My answer was, "But sir, I don't work here." He asked, "You don't? Would you like a job?" My stammering answer was, "Yes, I guess so."

Mr. Helms took me up to the office ahead of all those people applying for work and signed me up to work for Sears Roebuck. I still carry the same Social Security Card that was issued to me that day. Needless to add here, I did not join the Navy. I worked for Sears Roebuck. The joke made its way around that the Store manager could not fire me because I had been hired out of the main office in Chicago by the Vice President of Sears.

After several months on the third floor assembling furniture and toys and making repairs here and there I was offered a job in the service department. My primary work there was servicing automobiles. I was in charge of mounting new tires, batteries and changing oil etc. I liked that job much better but I still was not satisfied. That would not be my stopping place. However, it did turn my life in my desired direction.

I was most fortunate to have a very good job during the hard times of the great depression. I found a cheap apartment at Miss Billingsly boarding house on Lamar Street only a few blocks away. It amounted to being a small bedroom up a ladder into the attic through a hinged trap door. The bath room I was offered to use was on the second floor, also used by several other boarders. Miss Billingsly was especially nice to me. She promised to let me have the first room to be available on the first or second floor. The meals, served three times a day, were very good. The older lady who did the cooking was especially nice. If I came in late in the evening, and I often did, she would make me a special dish or two of whatever I wanted. She seemed to be waiting up for me when I would came in late.

OLD THUNDER

From the time my great Uncle, Moses Kierce (Grandma Harper's brother) let me ride with him in his 1923 T-Model Ford to Alvord and back, I lived for the day when I could have my very own automobile. That day came with my Sears Roebuck job in 1936. When I figured my budget I could pay $5 a month payments and still have enough money left to buy gasoline—sort of. Those were the early days of buying on credit and the time limit was no more than six months. I do not recall how much the interest rate was. However much – that would be tacked onto my payment. So the automobile I could buy would have to cost no more than $35. I found a used 1926 model Chrysler sedan that would run. The price tag was $50 but it was on special for only $35. For the first time in my life I went into debt.

The old Chrysler was like an 8-foot long, 5-foot wide and 6-foot high cracker box with the 5-foot long motor cowling the shape of a tomato can on top of two front wheels, with fenders covering each wheel and a running board in between on both sides. It was purchased new by an oil magnet named Carter McGregor in 1920 for the ridiculous price of $1,200. It had a front and back seat with coiled springs, padded covering of genuine leather with tie-down buttons. The windows had straps by which the glass could be pulled up and let down. It had a windshield wiper operated by a crank on the inside. The floor boards were a bit *gappy*. One could watch the ground passing beneath while riding down the road. It had the latest in hydraulic brakes; however, they never did work, so I had to depend on the emergency brake for stopping. The man at the used car lot started it for me and I drove it back to the boarding house and parked it and had to save for three months to buy a new battery before I could get it started again. Once I could start my fancy Chrysler, I was determined to drive it back to Lake Valley and show my dad how prosperous I had become. Being a fast learner, I soon learned how expensive my new old car was to drive. It took almost as much oil as it did gas to show off my wealth.

Old Thunder (That is what I called my new second-hand Chrysler) sounded extra loud when cranked up because it had no muffler and very little exhaust pipe. The sound it made reminded me of a rolling thunder storm with large hail. Old Thunder was also a mite tricky to drive. I had to drive with one hand on the steering wheel and the other on the emergency brake. Fortunately, back then the traffic was not like it is now. Stopping Old Thunder required a system of planning. At twenty miles per hour (estimated because the speedometer didn't work) it took about one hundred yards to stop. A safe distance to drive behind the car in front was best at a half mile. The headlights were non-functional but the tail light did light up some of the time. Usually it just sputtered on and off so it was wise not to drive it after dark.

I had a strange interest in girls in those days and decided early on that a trial run in Old Thunder was in the offing. I did this run around Old High about 4 o'clock one Friday evening. The horn didn't work so I tried wagging my windshield wiper but not any of the girls noticed. About that time I heard this triple-decker-horn blasting out a loud musical middle C chord. I never dreamed I would have such competition. Well, here came Clint Friberg in his fancy "Straight Eight Cord Convertible." That automobile had everything: not only those great chromium horns mounted out on the left front fender, it also had two fender-wells with spare tires and covers that advertised B. F. Goodrich Tire and Rubber Company. I had never seen the likes before. That slick Cord had a chromium radiator cap with a mermaid streaming out front. There was a rumble seat and the top let down. The color was fire-engine-red with a white, double racing-stripe full length on both sides—Wow! Old Clint didn't just pick up one girl he picked up half a dozen.

The next few hours of my time off were spent working on the old horn, and finally I heard a slight beep which encouraged me to work on it some more later. I cleaned the old thing up by scrapping off a bunch of rust. It was in no way like Clint's big three trumpet job, but it worked. It was not a very healthy sound - more like a bull frog with laryngitis. I finally had a horn to honk.

Eventually, I did pick up this nice young senior. I will call her Ima Broadbottom (not her real name but it fits the profile). She informed me upon entering my vehicle, "I am a nice girl, I am." She was somewhat fluffy. The broad front seat of Old Thunder seemed to close in when she embarked. I had to have her try crossing her legs, if possible, so that I could get to the emergency brake. I was afraid I might get her dress-tail hung up in the system. That might cause her to consider me not to be a nice man. I took Ima home but could never remember her address — but she never forgot mine.

The next day after my encounter with Miss Broadbottom I had barely returned to Ms. Billings Boarding House, bathed and dressed for dinner, when I heard this loud "BEEEP, BEEEP, BEP—BEP— BEP." Ima had borrowed her father's Model A Touring car and come to **pick me up**. Naturally, conditions being as they were, I had to decline her unusual come-on, and she drove sadly away. That was the end of that; or was it? The next day, about an hour later than the day before; bath, dress, dinner all finished, again this BEEEP, BEEEP, BEP—BEP—BEP. I sighed despondently and looked over at Ms. Billings. She smiled with a motherly smile and asked, "Would you like for me to get rid of her for you?" My immediate response was in the affirmative. She did.

After Ima Broadbottom, I scheduled my girly pickup hopes to a parking place in front of Allison's Drug Store. That was the center of civilization on Saturday evening back in the early days, before television. Everybody went down town on Saturday. What we called **having fun** in those days was not something that would destroy our virginity and cause us to spend the rest our lives wondering why. I had witnessed some fellows having pick-up luck there, so I parked early in order to have the favorite spot smack-dab in front. I laid the cause of my <u>no luck</u> on my funny looking old car. When I would *toot* my funny horn *the* girls would stop, look, giggle and go on down the street. A few giggles later, I returned to the boarding house and went to bed. O well, those ignorant girls didn't know that I had a good job working at Sears. If they had only known? If only.

Old Thunder was not the most reliable transportation one could hope for, and for sure it did not attract females. I found a much newer model Chevrolet Coupe that might do a better job for me. The price was $200. Old Thunder was worth $25 as junk so it only cost me $175 plus tax and interest. I don't recall just how much all of that come to but I could still eek out enough money for payments, gas and board. I found another place where I could hang my hat; it came with a private bath (sort of) and make my own bed and do my laundry. I would need to eat out but could cut down on the eats and save a little on the side. I was still dreaming of Miss Right.

It was not long after my new service job that I met another gentleman who would play a major role in my life. Mr. John Bradley Dollard drove his old Essex car in and needed a battery. I installed the new battery, explained the warranty and there got acquainted with a good man who was destined to one day cross my path again.

A few months later my Sears employment was interrupted by a telephone call from my very distant cousin, my Great Uncle Moses Kierce's grand son. One, Mr. William (Bill) Lee called me from Fort Worth to explode my plans once more. Bill had struck it rich and I must come and share in his tremendous opportunity. Why I listened and then followed is another mystery. How could I be so naive? He was sending his younger brother to Wichita Falls. I would need to get him my good job at Sears. — Would I recommend him? Well, his brother, whom I knew to be a good and honest man had the personality of a wide eyed Comanche warrior. Although he was a good and honorable person his looks would not recommend him favorably. I should have been inundated with red flags at this point but I was not. I turned my apartment over to him and took him to my place of employment recommending him for my replacement. After loading all of my belongings into my automobile, I headed for Lake Valley where I left my car for my sister Zula Belle and Papa to use as they needed, then caught the bus and proceeded on to meet Mr. Bill Lee in Fort Worth.

I suppose I have never been so thoroughly disappointed as when I learned the nature of the journey I had embarked upon, of all things, a door-to-door salesman. Once I had tried becoming a Fuller Brush *door to door* salesman, which I hated and flunked. Cousin Bill assured me that this was much more lucrative and If I would do it I could make 50 dollars a day or more. First I would need to learn how to be something of a scam artist. I would need to learn how to manipulate people into believing themselves to be winners. I was to hold up a dozen or so envelopes, fan them out just so and in one, just one, of those envelopes there just might be a prize, if the person was lucky. I was to make sure the person was lucky. Every one was to be a winner but the real winner would be the salesman if the manipulation was done convincingly. The prize was to be a favorite family photo, which the *lucky* winner, would bring out. It would be enlarged, and hand painted by a famous artist. Each salesman was provided with a large brief-case that did contain some beautiful examples set in expensive frames. This would be especially significant if the photo happened to be of a deceased parent or child. All of the flaws in the photograph could be corrected, a chosen background could be included. The down-payment would belong to the salesman and that was to be a rather lucrative price. The first percentage of the sale money was to go to my sponsor, who happened to be cousin Bill Lee. Then it was that I learned the rest of the story. The big money came when the delivery people unveiled the finished product. How could you say "no" to the high price of a gorgeous picture, framed under curved class, of a dearly beloved family member long deceased? This country kid, brought up to be up front in all my dealings could not bring myself to imbibe in such dubious chicanery. I immediately reached for a train ticket back to the hills of home.

Back to square one—no job. However, the Lord was with me once more. I landed another very good job back in Wichita Falls with The Willard Battery Co. which later become the Paulk Tire Company. Kindle and Irene Paulk were good to me. Irene must have realized that I was destined for more than the dirty manual labor of servicing automobiles. She gave me a pocket size dictionary knowing that I would need to enlarge my vocabulary if I were to amount to anything in the business world. I never did talk to anybody about my dream of higher education. During this period of time I had completely dismissed my life long dream of becoming a Christian Minister. In fact I had willingly disassociated my life from the church. I was an agnostic.

MY LOVE STORY

As a boy I often dreamed of the girl I would some day marry. There was never any question in my mind what she would be like. I seemed to have an instinctive vision of the girl I could love and honor "until death do us part." My favorite Aunt, Georgia Barns, had a little girl. I distinctly remember how cute she was and that my aunt named her Marie. That would be a nice name for my intended. That would be her name. That same small boy also dreamed that one day he would be a preacher. The most special role-model I had was a young Baptist preacher named Dale Thorn. He was well educated, a very spiffy dresser and drove one of the spiffiest cars to appear in our valley. He had a very pretty, petite and sweet little wife. She was a good piano player. That was nice, too. But my great concern was, "How do I get there from here?" My prayer, "Lord, You lead me and I will try to follow."

As a child, I delighted in arranging the dinning room chairs, and the old bench in rows like church pews. I would then summon my

three sisters and whoever else would come and be seated in my congregation and would proceed to preach to them. I do not recall any
of my first sermons but it seemed that being brought up in a devout
Baptist Church I had a terrible concept of the devil and how he made
us do bad things. That seemed to be the gist of my great Biblical
messages. On one such occasion, I recall my sister, Pauline, broke
out in tears. I just knew that I had arrived. That, supposedly, was
a sure sign that I had brought down the power of the Holy Spirit.
When I failed to drum up an audience of people to preach to I would
go out behind the barn, turn the old half-bushel bucket (used to measure corn) up-side-down and stand on it and preach to the chickens.
Occasionally a cow or two would wander into my sanctuary. We had
a bunch of cats. They should have been the most righteous cats in
the world for they gave me their undivided attention. Another thing I
learned that might help was that if I fed them, my attendance would
grow. I just loved it. But back to my love story: I needed a wife
who could play the organ. Dale Thorn's wife could play the old Este
Pump Organ and that was neat, I thought. Boy-hood passed and with
it a lot of "common fancies" but somehow, stored up in my memory
was that special someone that I must find.

Now, twenty years plus and still the right Marie who played the
organ hadn't materialized. Then one day it happened. Reading the
Wichita Daily Times, I saw the picture of a beautiful young lady.
The caption not only spelled out the right name "Marie" but also
that this one had just scored a victorious organ recital on one of the

big Highland Park Methodist Church Pipe Organs in Dallas. What a far-out idea that she would even look at me let alone get serious with me. But here, I hastened to cut out her picture and the article accompanying it, neatly folded it and tucked it away in my bill-fold. A year or so passed and nothing had come of my dream girl. My brother Roy and his son "Red" sang in the Scottish Rite Choir. I was invited to accompany them to their regular rehearsal. Taking a back seat, trying to be as inconspicuous as possible I settled into a ho-hum attitude that was to be short lived. The director of the Scottish Rite Choir was a Medical Doctor by the name of L. D. Parnell. He arrived with two of the most gorgeous young ladies; they were his accompanists at the piano. One was a blond, her name was Lucile Crouch. The other was a brunette and her name was Marie Dollard. I had arrived at last; except for one thing — they had dates with a couple of Aggie with brown boots. I was never good at competition. O well, so much for that. I was then employed at the Willard Battery Company as an installation and maintenance person. One morning sometime later I was attending to my boring occupation and heard the summon for a battery at what to me had become a familiar address, "1213, Taylor Street." I had often "walked down that street before." What if? O if only! They needed a battery, post haste. Our emergency calls were usually made by my old working buddy "Rosy." My immediate response: dropping what ever it was I was doing, and collaring Rosy, demanding, "I'll take that call." I arrived post-haste at 1213 Taylor Street, screeched up into the driveway and behold — there she stood —

waiting patiently for someone to install a rental battery in her father's old Essex. I recognized that old car as one in which I had installed a new battery a year or so earlier for a man named J. B. Dollard. I became so excited that I not only put the battery in backward, I also left some of my tools. She was everything I had dreamed she would be, plus the startling realization that her father was a man with whom I was already acquainted. I found that I wasn't exactly a stranger. I remembered that there was a good movie on at the Strand Theater that night so I immediately asked if she would go with me. She said she would like to but that her Uncle Gus Byman had died and they were preparing to attend the funeral, perhaps some other time—and I made that sooner than later. I scored a hit. I had finally arrived.

John B. Dollard

Marie's father, J. B. Dollard, was bedfast at this time. He was a finish carpenter by trade, but was not able to work. He had owned a good number of rent houses around town. Rent from those rent houses was to be his retirement income. During the Great Depression he was unable to keep them rented or to collect the rent from those that were rented. When tax time came around he was unable to pay so the county repossessed all but the one at -1213 Taylor, and sold them for taxes. J. B. was emotionally crushed. He was pathetic. I felt so sorry for him. On top of all that, he had been involved in an accident where a car had run over his right foot and had broken all the bones in his foot. Then, to cap it all off; the stress he had endured had caused him to develop stomach ulcers. Some doctor had told him the lining in his stomach was all gone. J. B. took this to be a death sentence. He gave up all hopes of ever recovering.

J. B. Dollard was one of the nicest, kindest and most gentle men I have ever known. I also loved him. He, in many ways, was like the father I had wished my own father to be. In his helpless condition it had become necessary for his little wife to take in washing and do house work for the neighbors and Marie was having to spend many hours, days and nights playing accompaniment for dance studios and voice teachers to provide a living for her ailing parents. Marie, at this time was also the Assistant Pipe-Organist at Floral Heights Methodist Church. She was studying organ under Mrs. A. H. Mahaffey who was the Organist at Floral Heights Methodist Church.

It was very early in the year 1937 Marie was called to be the Organist at First Christian Church. Mrs. Dudley Strange had been the first organist to serve First Christian. She had served during the installation of the first Pipe Organ. Marie would be the second Organist of the Church. I shall never forget how insecure Marie felt playing organ accompanimets under the very, stern Music Director, Martha Holms. I made it a point at first, to go with her when she went to practice on the Big Organ. She felt so alone, and worried. Fortunately, Martha Holms was understanding and helpful to her. They became close friends in time.

Naturally, Marie and her mother loved having me help them. I would start to work early enough to go by and help J. B. with his bath and shaving each morning. It gave Marie and me time and opportunity to get really well acquainted, which was all right with me. Her father's old Essex was not dependable transportation so I would have her drive me to work and keep my car to use for her activities. This went on for the better part of two years. That led to proposal and setting of our wedding date. It was to be the following June 14, 1938. It would be necessary to have a simple home wedding since neither of us had any spare money. We would drive back to my family home in Lake Valley. My father was an ordained minister by that time. He would do our ceremony. My sister Zella would be Marie's Matron of Honor and my nephew C. B. (red) Harper would be my Best Man. My little niece, Margaret Ellen Magness would play "Here Comes The Bride" on the old pump organ. My sisters had gone out and picked wild flowers for decoration and my mother and sisters had prepared a most delicious wedding dinner. It was an inexpensive affair but Marie and I remembered it with much fondness and could not have hoped for anything nicer. To us it was perfect.

Regrets? There were some. Marie had saved up enough money to give me a very nice wedding ring. I was so strapped for money the only thing I could afford was a tiny gold wire-ring that cost me $2. I was ashamed of it but it was the best I could do. I can never forget the disappointed look in her eyes when I slipped that little cheap thing on her finger. I promised her that I would replace it with a nicer one, but the big moment was lost forever. She was such a gracious, wonderful person. She never complained.

It was necessary that I be back at work the next morning. Marie and I had to leave shortly after that great wedding dinner. I don't recall that I ever told my family how much I appreciated what they did to make our wedding a memorable occasion. I remember how proud I was of my neat, shiny 33 Plymouth coup; our transportation vehicle. I had had it refinished with racing stripes and white-wall tires. Likely, the money I spent on my car should have been used to purchase a suitable wedding ring. Marie loved my Plymouth coupe.

CHANGE IN CHURCH MEMBERSHIP

M y church membership was still in the Lamar Baptist Church. Roy Harper, my older brother, was the choir director there. I was interested in singing in the choir. My older sister and her family were members there and it had seemed to be the thing for me to do to join Lamar Baptist with other members of our family. It was a much larger congregation than the Lake Valley Baptist Church. Four of the young men from the Sunday School class I attended were dedicated to study for the ministry. But, somehow I didn't feel that I was a part of their world and certainly did not share their enthusiasm. They were sent off to Baylor University in style. The whole congregation gathered around their fine automobile with prayers and well wishes. I thought it was very spectacular but not for me. Maybe it was envy. It never struck me as the kind of humility one should have for such a sacred trust as Christian Ministry.

An accumulation of small but serious happenings caused some concern for me. There were some things going on that I could not identify as being Christian. I was acquainted with some of the deacons of Lamar Church out in the business world whose action turned me off. That could have been my problem but I, nonetheless allowed it to turn me away from the church for a long period of time. If I understand the meaning of agnosticism, *if there is a god, he is not concerned about human life,* then I was an agnostic. All dreams of becoming a Christian Minister were history. Little did I realize that even under those horrendous conditions I was still being lead by the Holy Spirit.

Psalm 139:7-10

"Whither shall I go from thy spirit?
Or whither shall I flee from thy presence?
If I ascend up into heaven, thou art there:
If I make my bed in hell, behold thou art there.
If I take the wings of the morning and dwell in the uttermost parts of the sea;
Even there shall thy hand lead me and thy right hand shall hold me..........."

After Marie became the organist at First Christian it seemed to be clear that she should place her membership there. I had not been attending church anywhere since losing faith in Lamar Baptist

Church. But I began attending the Christian Church. Dr. O. L. Shelton was minister. For the first time in my life I began to hear the Christian Gospel as I had never heard it before. Attending church became something I yearned to do. Sunday School took on a meaningful place in my life for the first time. My dream of becoming a minister bubbled up in my dreams once more but the same dark cloud of doubt still dimmed my future. If I was to reach as high as my dreams continued to insist, I must have an academic ladder to climb on. How can I get there from here?

It was in 1942 that my son John Curtis was born. That probably was one of the really happy times in my memory. After Marie recovered from her very difficult delivery, things leveled out for a while. I had a very good job, considering my ability to perform. There never seemed to be enough money. I moved from job to job, to job always realizing I needed to get back to finishing school some way. I was employed at the Panhandle Refining Company at that time. The pay was much better than any job I had ever had before. The pay was.75 cents an hour. The work was simple and easy; laboratory work, cracking still, blending tank, general yard maintenance, construction, all very interesting but not fulfilling for me. The refinery went the same way as many factories and businesses had gone - ka-bust. After my days with the refinery I worked for a short time with the Empire Paper Company, driving the city delivery truck. I liked that better because it provided me much more opportunity to associate with people.

The old Texas Electric Service Gang. (I'm in the center, holding my hat)

It was in or about 1940 the clouds of World War II were beginning to form on the horizon. Shepherd Air force Base was becoming very busy. It became necessary that the electric system at Shepherd Field be up-graded. I applied for and received a job with Texas Electric Service Company, Transmission Department. My first job was helping to construct a larger transmission line from the transformer yard to Shepherd. In those days holes for the power poles were dug with rather primitive tools compared to today's equipment. With a hand auger, a long handle spade, a spoon, and a rock-bar we had to dig holes at least 5 foot deep on those rock infested hills between Wichita Falls and Shepherd. There was a lot of tough digging. Some of the holes would take an entire 8 hour day and then some to complete. After the new 66 KVA line was finished they gave me a job as Transmission Line Dispatcher. In fact I was frozen on that job for the duration of the war. For the first time in my life, I felt that I was doing something worth while. The job I held with the Electric Power Company was as good as it could get for someone without a college degree. The pay was fair and the future was very good but I still longed for something more fulfilling. I had dreamed of Christian Ministry for so many years I was unable to be content with only a good job and a financial future. There surely had to be something better.

OPTIMIST CLUB

Otto Kitterman, Lloyd Yarbrough, Me and Jim Jacobsen The Optimist Four barbershop quartet.

B ack in the mid 1940s I was privileged to be a part of the original group of men to organize the Optimist Club in the city of Wichita Falls. We found a good meeting place in the Kemp Hotel. Jim Jacobsen, Max Krutz, Otto Kitterman and I made up the first members of the Optimist Quartet; Later, Lloyd Yarbrough took the place of Max Krutz. Lloyd was a great show-man. He had been an entertainer on Radio Station WBAP, Dallas as "Captain Apple Blossom" for many years prior to his being moved by the railroad company, with which he was employed as freight agent, to Wichita Falls. This was also in the very early days of radio. He was a folk singer with his old four stringed "whatever - he called it a Bo-jing;" I believe it tuned more like a Mandolin or perhaps a Yuka-la-la. What ever, he could really make it sing.

We used male quartet music in those days. We had not, as then been informed about the *Society for the Preservation and Encouragement of Barber Shop Quartet Singing in America Incorporated.* (SPEBSQSA Incorporated) that came after I had spent some time on a business trip to Springfield, Massachusetts. It was in the ending days of WW2, I was invited to stay in the home of Mr. William Crain. His family originated the Crain Manufacturing Company there in Springfield (they built all kinds of porcelain bath fixtures. In our usual conversation one morning around the breakfast table I happened to mention my interest in quartet singing. He, too, was a music lover and asked me if I had heard about the SPEBSQSA. I had not. He told me the story about its origin in the basement of the Mulebock Hotel in Kansas City, Kansas. Incidentally, I later stayed at the Mulebock and saw the bronze plaque fixed on a column in the basement. Mr. Crain gave me an envelope with the address of SPEBSQSA and I wrote them and they sent me the literature that provided the necessary connections to start our own Organization.

We organized and received our first Barber Shop music arrangements in the mid 1940's. It was great. I remember how much pleasure we received from singing that marvelous close-harmony music. Yarborough was first tenor, Kitterman was second tenor, I did baritone and Jim Jacobsen did the base. We performed for many affairs, advertising our Optimist Club. One of the missions of the club was to *always be ready to assist fellow Optimist Members in time of trouble.* I remember very well one occasion, one of our fellow Optimists, Rabby Hampton, of the Hampton and Vaughn Funeral home, had a most serious heart rending experience. For reasons unknown to me Rabby's wife left him. He was really down. Yarbrough, Kitterman, Jacobs and myself spent an entire Sunday evening and night with him in his home. We sang and drank a few high-balls and kept Mr. Hampton busy all night until he finally fell asleep. To the best of my memory his wife relented and came back so that all was well at the Hampton house. So much for the Optimist Quartet.

Much later, Lloyd Yarborough's Son, Dan, followed me into Christian Ministry. He is now retired and lives in Pensacola Florida. Lloyd retired in the late 1940's and moved to Missouri. He had plans to build a center for entertainment. I have never been sure but believe he had much to do with The Branson, Missouri fling we hear so much about. Otto Kitterman died back in the 1950s. Jim Jacobs who at that time was band director of, what is now Midwestern State University in Wichita Falls, later advanced to become Band Director at Texas Christian University in Fort Worth, Texas.

I was still praying 'Lord, are you still listening? I need your guiding Spirit. Tell me, how can I get where I need to be?"

Perhaps I could start a business and have something ready for some returning veteran. Just perhaps I could amass enough money to pursue my dream of completing my education. During the war, gasoline and tires were rationed. I more or less parked my great little Plymouth Coupe. Marie could use it to do her thing. I found a used bicycle for $15. That would have to be my transportation to and from the office. Peddling a bike was not my preference for transportation. A vehicle with a motor was on my preference list. Sure enough that prayer was heard. A young man who lived up in the next block offered to trade me a motorcycle for my bicycle. Sounded like an excellent idea. Only one thing—the motor was in a wash-tub. He assured me it was all there. It just needed to be reassembled, with some new parts which I would have to find. I was always a good scrounger and fixer-upper so that would be no problem for me. In the meantime, I fell in love with motorcycles. Not only was it good, cheap transportation, it was fun. To make a long story shorter, as soon as it was available, I purchased myself a new Indian Chief (a police model). A big mistake! I would now need to go into the Motorcycle Business. That would be the business I could sell out and have my college money. Boy! Was my world shaping up. I then began to dream big.

As soon as the war was ended I took it on. The first thing I began to do was order up some franchises. They were available. First, the

Indian Motorcycle Company. Next, I was attracted to the RV world. Winnebago Company had just come out with a first rate line of RVs for North Texas and Southern Oklahoma territory—yeh. Next, the Casrtrol motor oil franchise was open. So was Haveline Motor Oil (now, a General Motors oil). I got lined up with a Sports Wear Company. I had it made in the shade. All I needed was time and money. Sadly, I ran out of both. My aptitudes for the business world were as likely as my ability to fly a Boeing 747. I knew exactly nothing about running a business. Now I know. Then it was that I learned. I once tried the Ranching Business. I blew that one as well. More about that latter.

My borrowed money ran out and business went flat. Times grew more difficult. Creditors were barking at me at every turn. With the sheriff looking for me. I had to run. I wasn't about to fold. In the first place, the money I had been spending I learned, was ill gotten money and innocently, I was doing a "money laundering job" for a bootlegger. The, not-exactly-nice, money man had sicked the sheriff on me. It is not always what you know that is as great as who you know. "Hey! Cousin, J. Walter Friberg, help."

Fortunately Mr. Friberg was well acquainted with the situation. Old Walter was, himself, a pretty heavy drinker at one time. And as the old saying goes, "What hits the fan is not always evenly distributed." My cousin, now a lawyer, the All Wise Attorney, J. Walter Freiberg, was quick to inform the bootlegging man that his future would have much more freedom if he left town post haste. And that, he did, so my case cooled considerably. The sheriff just smiled and walked away. Wow! That was close! My financial situation was exactly zilch. What will I do for an encore?

MY FIRST CHURCH JOB

First Christian Church in Wichita Falls, Texas (Courtesy of First Christian Church)

D r. Doug McCall, our minister at First Christian learned about my predicament and called for me to come to his office. "Would I like to take an interim job as Youth Director, since Al. Holt had vacated the job." Am I dreaming? Is this real? Wow! Would I!

From that day until this things undreamed of have opened for me. I learned much latter on that my behest was the subject of hundreds of prayers offered up by those wonderful folk at First Christian Church. How could I fail in my new direction?

With my first paycheck from the church, after the necessary bills were paid and groceries bought, I had barely enough money left to buy a round trip train ticket to Fort Worth and Texas Christian University. I would check out my possibilities of furthering my much prayed for education. I had to walk from the train station all the way out to T.C.U. No bus fair. I managed to make the rounds. From window to window and office to office. Not much encouragement there. While I was walking back across the campus alone and dejected, I happened to meet a professor I had met during the summer youth conference at Mineral Wells, Dr. William Reid. His first question, "What are you doing here?" I told him my story. He invited me to walk with him to his home. His wife prepared a sandwich for us. It was the first food I had tasted all day. We talked until about time for me to catch the train back to Wichita Falls. Dr. Reid assured me that I was doing the right thing and that he would help me in every ways possible.

Back home again; Marie and I talked about our future hopes. Our plans were not yet in recognizable perspective. Actually, Marie felt that it was hopeless. The only argument I had was: "The Lord will provide." With that, I went to sleep and had my first restful night in recent memory.

MY FIRST CHURCH IN MORAN

Moran Christian Church

The next morning after a good breakfast with my family there were some chores around the house that needed my attention. It would be necessary for me to walk from 1213 Taylor to Tenth and

Travis. I had some things I needed to do around the church, then I would go up to Dr. McCall's office and clear my plans with him.

Dr. McCall received me with his usual warm greeting. He asked me, "How are things going?" He did not know that I had been to Fort Worth and TCU. Without hesitation I announced to him, "I am going to enroll in TCU this fall."

His startled reply was, "You are going to what?"

I repeated my announcement. Doug leaned back in his big chair and asked softly, "How are you going to do that? It takes money to go to college. You don't have the money. You don't have your high school diploma, how on earth could you ever get into a great school like Texas Christian University?"

My answer, "I will have to pass their entrance exam. I will need to get a student church and preach my way through."

Dr. McCall, with the hint of a smile on his face, his pale blue eyes half closed in contemplation looked at me for a long moment. I could almost read his thoughts, "Dumb idiot, what can I say."

I thought to ease his concern, "I believe the Lord will somehow make it all possible."

"Yea, sure," was his reply. At that precise moment his secretary interrupted, "Dr. McCall, Mrs. White, the State Secretary for the CWF is on line one."

Dr. McCall slowly picked up the phone and responded as usual. He listened for a couple of moments, turned pale, looked up at me, and literally dropped the phone in his lap.

Doug McCall shook his head slowly for a moment and retrieved the phone, looked up at me again and very distinctly told the lady, "I have one standing right here." Then with a wide smile, he lowered the phone and said, "Mrs. White is calling from our church in Moran. They need a minister to begin next Sunday. Would you like to take that one?"

Then it was that I, almost collapsed with joy. "Sure that is my calling. I'll try-out Sunday."

Doug then informed me that Moran is a little town in Shakelford, County — 15 miles south of Albany, Texas, in wild ranch country, with no public transportation for miles. "How are you going to get there? You don't have a car." Dr. McCall observed.

Again, my answer, "I believe the Lord will provide." This time he again slowly shook his head with that questioning smile. "Sure, Sure!"

I went car shopping. I didn't have even the price of a gallon of gas, as a matter of fact all I had was faith. I did not know what to expect, if anything, but I knew there were things going on in my behalf that were beyond understanding.

The very first place I came to was this used car lot with a sign that read: THE WALKING MAN'S FRIEND. I, there met a man who would prove to be a friend indeed, Otis Thomas, a retired Texas Ranger. I told him my story. Sure, he would work with me. "I have this old car over here, not the best looking car on the lot but a good one. A 1936 Nash-Lafayette. It has an over-drive and will get good gas mileage. I have $200 in it and you can have it for that amount and repay me when you are able."

This was the beginning of a legend. I named the old Nash-Lafayette "Jezebel." That ugly, beat-up old car turned out to be one of the most remarkable automobiles I ever owned. It continued to be, all the way through my BA degree and well into my first years in graduate studies. What a deal!

Years later, while serving our church in Vernon, Texas I was to meet Otis Thomas again. He was a close friend of Lester Boyd who was a member of my church there. Otis Thomas made a statement of simple logic that explained my unusual experience most clearly. "You can't take a wrong step in the right direction."Otis Thomas has been dead for years now, but I still honor his memory. He was a tough old Texas Ranger but a good Christian man at heart.

Back for a moment with my old Nash-Lafayette. It did have some problems that demanded attention. When I first received it I sought to revitalize it with some additives which I placed into the gas-tank and into the motor-oil. Additives that were meant to clean and free up the piston rings, valves and what-ever. The additives had loosed a lot of sludge in the oil pan. This sludge, as one would expect, needed to be cleaned out of the oil pan. My time and money being fully allocated I chose to drive with one eye on the oil gauge. When I saw the oil gauge begin to drop I would take the motor out of drive and let the sump fill with fresh oil. As soon as the sump was replenished and the pressure came back up I would continue to tack the motor again.

This was a bit inconvenient but it worked, that is until one Saturday I was on my way to Moran. It was raining. I was climbing one of those long hills in Eastland County, almost to the top, when the oil-pressure zeroed out and I failed to rescue the tack in time. "Rattle-clang-bang and stall," the old motor swarmed on me.

"What do I do now, Lord? Do you have any more miracles for me or is that it? Lord are you paying attention? It is raining harder now than ever. What am I going to do?"

"Well yes, try the starter." I stepped on the starter and to my utter amazement it started. It didn't exactly run good but it did run. It had about four cylinders that were working. It was enough to finish my journey. After the morning service I informed the folks I would need to continue on to Wichita falls while it was day. With a few quarts of oil to burn I managed to limp back to my man in Wichita Falls. Monday morning I was back to see Otis Thomas. Yes, he knew a mechanic who could fix it for me. "Just leave it here and I will take care of it for you." Thanks again Otis. See you on Friday.

Can you imagine an old six cylinder engine, with the top completely blown on the number one piston. Number two piston was minus a couple of ring lands. The cylinder wall on number two was scored but not so badly as to prevent it from serving for a while. The mechanic managed to find another old Nash Junker and retrieved a couple of pistons that would serve me for a while. He cleaned up the oil sump and strainer. All of this for only $35?

Back to the beginning of my story.

Moran, Here I come. MY FIRST SERMON must have been a duzzy. It included many Biblical quotations, some really weird illustrations, even a lengthy Shakespearian thriller. My intention was to really knock'em over. Unfortunately, the reaction was a surprising "Ho hum." I thought, as we sang the hymn of Christian fellowship, "Lord are you paying attention? I blew it, darn it! See what you can do about it."

I was invited to remain for a brief board meeting after the last amen. Bertrand Elliot, probably one of the richest, oiliest old rancher in Shackelford County, the head elder, was the first to speak. "Poor preach poor pay but his sincerity seems real. What do you fellows think?" I received an arousing ya. "Lord, I don't know how you did it but thanks again." I was in! The salary would be $37.50 a week. I would have a morning and evening service. My presence would be expected on Saturday and Sunday and at such occasions as emergencies might require. I could handle that.

MY LIFE AT TCU

My next hurdle could be the highest of them all. "Please Lord, have mercy on your stupid servant." <u>The College Entrance Examination</u> would cause me to loose much sleep. I would need all the proof of schooling I could find. I had audited two semesters in Harden College (now called Midwestern State University). That might help. I went to the, then, superintendent of the Alvord high school. He was able to, not only encourage me but also to provided a letter of recommendation that helped greatly in processing my application for enrollment into the TCU Baccalaureate program. I wasn't ready, I admitted to myself but it was going to happen, ready or not, on the following Monday morning.

I arrived at TCU that morning, bright and early, with fear and trembling. After spending all night in prayer I was still a mite anxious. The gentleman who was to be in charge of my exam got there about the same time I arrived. His first words to me were, "I have never met you but I feel that I know you. My wife attended grade school with you in the Lake Valley school. She was Maureen Davis, the grand-daughter of Mr. Jim Harry who purchased your grand-father Miller's old farm. Maureen sends her regards." What is this, Lord? Another miracle?

He asked me to relax for a moment over a cup of coffee. I am sure he was noticing how up-tight I was. He then assured me he would help me as much as he could, which turned out to be a considerable amount. Somehow, that kind, wonderful man managed to find me a passing grade. His last advice to me was very wise also. "Find out which classes the foot-ball scholar-ship boys are taking and sign up." Wow, was that a great idea! I have never again knowingly laid eyes on the man who nurtured me through that test and gained my entrance into that great institution. I do not know his name. What a pity. I owe him so much. Texas Christian University was, and is a most difficult University into which to gain entrance and as I was to learn, even more difficult to get out of. The last class reunion I attended the speaker referred to me, joking: "Harpo didn't enroll in TCU, he homesteaded."

I was to be further blessed by First Christian Church, Wichita Falls by receiving a Ministerial Scholarship. $4 a semester hour was still scary but it was possible even with my terrible financial experience. I would pour out my need to a loan-officer at the Herring Bank, Fort Worth. It worked. I could pay it back with two or more payments.

Also, at the beginning of each semester I would receive a check from a bank in Wichita falls. It was a simple casher check, anonymous. I never knew for sure but I have a feeling those checks came from the Kevel Class, First Christian Church. Marie and I would visit Uncle Amyl Freiberg on occasion. Each time we started to leave Uncle Amyl would say to his wife, "Trudy, get the check book." I do not remember how many of those $100 checks he gave us but there were six or more. "The Lord did provide."

I would be living on the second floor in the old Reed House, a rather dilapidated old two story wooden structure. The old Reed House was referred to around the campus as "The Fish-Bowl." (Freshmen were called Fish) It was torn down in 1949 and the new Bright Divinity School was erected where it stood. The old fish-bowl was not a choice place to hang my hat but neither are beggars choosers. It would have to do until I could do better. Marie and John would have to remain in Wichita Falls for a while until we could come up with a better arrangement. After a month or so I was able to move Marie and John into the fish-bowl with me.

I surely must have been stepping in the intended direction. Doors began to open that I did not know existed. My weekly salary from the Moran Church was never quite enough to cover all of my expenses. One cup of coffee and a donut was hardly enough to sustain a 180-pound body all day. A minister friend and his wife who also lived in the old Reed House, like myself were having money problems. He had a contract with an apartment complex owner to clean and repaint vacated apartments. I went to work with him. I had not had any seminary training at this time. Every Sunday called for two sermons. Cleaning and painting apartments required six to eight hour days. I was attending four class periods, three in the morning and one in the afternoon, running a bit short on study time. It was a busy time but I loved it. Marie was still playing organ for First Christian. We needed that extra pay check. They were having choir rehearsals on Sunday evenings. She was commuting by train and bus Saturday and Sunday each week. It must have been a terrible ordeal for her but she never complained.

Sermon preparation time kept growing shorter and shorter. Soon my sermons were being mentally inscribed while driving to Moran on Saturday afternoons. I became very proficient in "off-the-cuff" oratory. I recall that on the day we were scheduled to do "impromptu speeches' my drama class, I had a face full of the mumps and had to miss that class. My son, John brought the mumps home from his school. The first class session after I recovered, the students themselves insisted on providing me with a subject. I was asked to speak, impromptu, for at least ten minutes on the subject "How to Vulcanize a Snake." I must have satisfied the requirement. Later the speech professor asked if I would represent TCU in Austin at the State level, Oratorical Competition. My answer was, "Sorry but I just don't have time to memorize a speech." He answered, "Memorize a speech? When have you ever memorized a speech?" I managed to slip out of that one.

Before leaving the "Fish Bowl," (the old Reed House) I have one more memory to share. There was a freshman by the name of Tom Schuster, a young single man, as I recall, from Pennsylvania. Tom was also studying for Christian Ministry. He was a strange one indeed. Apparently he owned nothing but the clothes he wore. He was assigned a room on the second floor of the Reed House. There were four rooms on the second floor. The other two were vacant. There was one bath that was to be shared by all of the second floor residents. It had four towel racks and four separate cabinets for toilet articles, shaving equipment, dental supplies and such. I came in one evening to bathe and found my towel wet and thrown over the side of the bathtub. O, no, Tom must have thought it was his. I went to my toiletry cabinet and discovered that my razor had been used and put back dirty. My toothbrush was in the slot but it was wet and had a bit of toothpaste on it. I was fit to be tied. I almost lost what little religion I had arrived with. What was I to do?

I gathered up everything I had in the bathroom and returned them to my room, except my bath mat. Fortunately I had two towels. I washed my soap-bar off, it had hair on it that was not blond. It too had been used. I bought myself a new toothbrush and cleaned my razor. After all of that I took my bath, brushed and shaved. This time I took all of my bathroom supplies back to my room. I had cooled off somewhat when Tom came in. I heard him prowling around in the bathroom. After his bath he came to my door dripping wet and complaining, "What did you do with <u>our</u> towel?" I informed him, that towel was mine, not our towel. "Well", he came back, "What did you do with that razor and tooth stuff?" I almost lost it, did some deep breathing—almost hyper ventilated. Finally my *cool* returned. I calmly informed Mr. Schuster that I was not responsible to furnish his bathroom needs. Would he mind leaving my things alone?

My friend Paul Thompson and wife lived on the first floor. They did their room up really nice, papered the walls with a rather expensive paper, even papered the ceiling, which was necessary on those old houses. When they went to bed that night, they were tired but proud of their newly decorated room. Low and behold, Tom Schuster came in late, turned on the water in the upstairs bath room, which was directly above the Thompson bed room, sat down and went to sleep. The bathtub ran over, right through the floor into the newly papered ceiling of the Thompson apartment and down came paper, water and all right on top of them in their bed. Needless to say Paul Thompson and wife were drenched in cold water, their bed was a soggy mess and they were two very unhappy campers.

Mr. Tom Schuster was not well loved around the campus. His days at TCU were cut short. He did not last through the first semester. One of his professors showed me a paper he had turned in. I could not read it. He would begin his sentences with little letters. He had presented a rather impressive high school diploma, which was thought to be a forgery, I was told. According to his professor he was one of the poorest students he had ever seen.

247

Once again a miracle, this time it was through the Seminary Dean, Dr. D. Ray Lindley. I could take the custodial responsibilities for the ministerial apartments and have my own apartment. Wow! Now I would have a place for Marie and John. I could move J.B. and Minnie into a Government Apartment. This was one of the happiest days of my life. No more painting apartments. More time for studying which I desperately needed.

My joys were 'diapered' however, when I opened the vacated apartment we were to occupy. The young couple that moved out had a baby. <u>Dirty Diapers everywhere</u>! A full corner of the bedroom was piled almost to the ceiling with dirty diapers. Instead of washing the diapers they would simply throw them in the corner on the pile. Two years of dirty diapers. They must have spent a fortune on new diapers. This was many years before disposable diapers were available. They would go out and buy a dozen more new cloth diapers. It would be difficult to imagine the terrible odor generated by those rotting, diapers. It took me many, many precious hours to clean up that horrible mess. Cleaning, scrubbing, deodorizing, repainting seemed to be an endless job. We were never able to completely eradicate the fowl odor. If one came into the apartment from out side and you could still smell the odor a year later. I was reminded that sanitation does not come natural for some preachers.

Marie was still doing the pipe organ for First Christian in Wichita Falls. She would commute by train on weekends. They would have choir rehearsal on Sunday evening and she would catch the bus back to Fort Worth Sunday, night. She would take John, our six year old son along with her. I don't know how she managed to do all of that. It must have been a terrible ordeal for her, but she never complained.

My B.A. minor was in Drama. I never dreamed that a course in drama would be so time consuming. We were scheduled to do a series of stage productions. I remember one especially. I had the leading role in an especially large cast for a great play entitled "Southern Exposure." I played the part of an elderly gentleman with gray hair. I recall how I had to use a lot of talcum powder to make the gray hair. The character I played was a pretty heavy drinker; I had fun with the stately boozy, older character. It was necessary to memorize a dozen or more pages of script. The performances were in the "Little Theater" behind the then new Ed Landreth Auditorium. As a matter of fact, the huge Ed Landreth stage served both Ed Landreth and Little Theater. The Little Theater would only seat about 150 people. We had a capacity crowd at most every evening's performance, as I recall.

And as if that was not enough I had also signed up to be the lead character in a 'Video Work Shop.' That was to be a weekly Television Production on Channel Five, Fort Worth; called 'The Dean of the College.' Playing the lead character, I would be on every set. The students were responsible for writing the script, doing the choreography, building the sets, finding the props. All of the lines had to be from memory. In those early days of TV there was no second chance. No taping; we performed live. Every thing went out on the air, the good and the goofs alike; consequently we spent many hours rehearsing. One wrong cue and the whole production could be a disaster. I there learned to cope with pressure. Discipline was a subject I had always been short of. I needed very much to stick to this study. It would do me good.

We would need to sell 1213, Taylor, Street, Wichita Falls, in order to be able to meet the needs of my in-laws in Fort Worth. The Taylor Street property did sell at the going price for such property at that time. I would later purchase a suitable property on Willing Street, east, south-east of TCU in what was then a new housing development. After a fair down payment, I took up a G.I. loan from the previous owner for a very good low-interest deal. We could move to the Willing Street property and I would no more need to serve as an apartment custodian. That would give more time to study. Thanks I needed that.

Our new Willing Street address was as comfortable as houses were in those days. It was less than two years old. There was no air conditioning in most houses back in the 1950s. The first thing I needed to do was to install an exhaust fan. I made a 24-inch square opening in the hallway ceiling. Then fitted it with an automatic grill cover that was held open by the suction from the fan and closed when the fan was turned off. There was a little factory on Berry street that made those grills. I worked about three weeks for the factory to pay for my exhaust fan and grill. That was the most drab job I ever had. I must have assembled two hundred or more of those pesky grills. The pay was small, as it was for all, "so called" unskilled labor jobs: 50 cents an hour. Jobs were scarce but pay checks were very necessary. The more fortunate of us were able to have more than one job. The more jobs the more pay checks we could have.

Eventually some of the professors came to know about my unusual work need and came to my aid. The Dean of Brite Seminary, Dr. D. Ray Lindley let me paint his house to pay for one whole year of tuition. There were jobs around the campus that I was able to do, like watering and setting out new trees, washing windows, mowing lawns. Not long ago a young lady from the Alumni office called me for the usual donations round up. She asked me how long ago it had been since I went to TCU. My answer, "You see those huge live oak trees up and down on both sides of University Drive? I planted them."

I served the Moran Church for about 18 months. It was a long drive that was consuming a lot of time and money but I came to love the people of Moran. It had proved to be the perfect place for me to 'break' into the Christian ministry. They were very supportive of my efforts and I felt I owed them a debt of gratitude.

It was at Moran where I did my first wedding. I shall never forget that Saturday night, November 1948. I had run out of money by Friday after purchasing enough gasoline to fuel Jezebel all the way to Moran and back Sunday evening. I was feeling a mite hungry, come Saturday noon but without money I didn't eat. I arrived in Moran about 12 o'clock noon. Perhaps I would get invited out to lunch. No such luck. I busied myself with my studies. Maybe the hunger will go away if I forget about it. I could look out the window and see the little café and could almost smell hamburger.

It was beginning to get dark. I had begun to think about going to bed early. The ladies had prepared for me a nice bedroom in a basement of the church. About that time I heard knocking on the front door of the church. I immediately answered the knock at the door. It was a young man. I took him to be a cowboy from one of the ranches, from his appearance. His first words were, "Would you marry us?" What I took to be the bride was seated in a pick-up truck out at the curb. I had already been coached not to perform weddings until I had had a chance to counsel the couple at least twice. But, overwhelmed with hunger, my immediate reply was, "sure. Bring the bride on in." Well, as it turned out it was not all that simple. They would need to go home and get ready and the family would be brought in. "Would 8 o'clock be all right?" "Sure that would be fine." The hamburger place stayed open until 10 o'clock on Saturday evenings. My mind was fixed on the wedding fee. How much money would he pay me?

This window of time would give me opportunity to go over the wedding ceremony. I ran down stairs, found my Worship Manual and opened it to the Wedding ceremony. My first wedding. Better read the whole thing over, I had plenty of time and must do everything according to the book.

The wedding party arrived on time. I went out to the curb to welcome them like a good pastor should. I noted immediately that the father of the bride was a bit tipsy. Regardless of his toxic condition I felt I must give him the opportunity to do the fatherly thing. Would he like to give the bride away? His slurred answer took me back for the moment, "Give her away? Hell he's already got her." That was the way it would be. I would have to delete that portion of the ceremony. No problem. The ceremony went according to the prescription. We had the "I do's" the rings and kissing. The wedding fee? I would take what ever he wanted to give me. Would it be a dollar, maybe two. It could be as much as five dollars. I had heard some were that generous. Finally, when I bid them God's speed and dismissed the party he shyly handed me fifty cents. I waited patiently until they all drove away and I headed for the café. Boy, was that burger ever good. Best hamburger I ever tasted. Cost a dime. I still had enough for a coke and a bar of candy. The end of a perfect day.

Moran would give me funeral conducting experiences. My first was a hard one. It was for a high school age young man. He had crashed his air plane not very far from the church. It was a DOA case. The family was wild with grief. I somehow managed to brave my way through. I am sure I was not the strong consoling pastor they desperately needed but I did my best.

My next funeral was one of the elders of the church. He was a rural mail carrier so it attracted a huge attendance. He was a comparatively young man, as I recall, in his early 60s. He left a wife, a daughter and a son and some grandchildren. I remember there were two or three more funerals while at Moran. They were all very difficult for me. I have always been emotionally inclined. I knew this had to be conditioning me for future service.

I had at least two other weddings while serving the Moran Church. Bertrand Elliot and wife, Grace became special to Marie and Me. As I mentioned before, Bertrand Elliot had one of the largest ranches in Shakelford, County. About every Sunday during fair-weather days they would have us come over to their ranch house for *steak dinner*. I don't know their secret but their steaks were like no other I hade eaten before or since: tender, delicious, perfectly seasoned and served hot off the griddle—wow! They always had fresh vegetables of about every kind. Fruit pies? Grace was the best chef I can remember.

VICKERY CHURCH IN DALLAS

A new opportunity opened for me and I felt the urge to step up. It was February 1950; it came to me as a divine provision with my name on it. Dr. Fred W. Carlock, an advanced student of Brite Divinity School was pastor of a church in Dallas. When he graduated from Brite he asked if I would be interested in going to the Dallas church as his replacement. The pay was much better and the distance was much shorter. It was also a much larger congregation. It seemed to be, for me, the perfect calling. It was the Vickery Christian Church, just off Greenville Avenue at Loop 12. Yes, I would offer them my services as pastor. And yes, once again, I was warmly accepted. They built a new parsonage next door to the church, trying to make life for my family as comfortable as possible. There again, I met some of the great people that brought much joy to my family and me.

The first Sunday morning after our being installed as minister of the Vickery church, I was surprised to have a man and wife whom I had considered to be older active members come forward for baptism. Their reason was that they had considered themselves to be members although they had never been baptized. They considered that I was the first minister they had had with whom they could feel comfortable receiving the sacred ordinance of Christian Baptism. I felt most humbled by that experience. It was a great place to live and work while receiving seminary classes.

1952 was the happiest, most eventful year in my early ministry. I not only received the college degree of my dreams, a month or so earlier Marie and I were once again parents of a baby boy. Robert Lowell (Bob) Harper was born on the third of July. We had been informed when John Curtis was born that there would be no more children for us. Marie had surgery before John was born that required one of her ovaries and half of the other to be removed. Both of our sons were miracle babies. Although Bob was a week or two premature, he was in great physical condition considering all the problems we encountered during the pregnancy.

The "Amazing Grace of God" was still opening doors for me. I look back on those days with a sense of awe. The way by which I had arrived is shrouded in mystery, like a wonderful dream that somehow came true. I was no more that naive, stupid, country kid from the sticks of Wise county but a true ministerial student moving up in a world that was now my own, a part of that great brother-hood of Christian Ministers, a divine calling that spans centuries of support for The Great Commission; *"Go ye therefore and make disciples of all nations, baptizing them in the name of the Father and of the Son and of the Holy Spirit, teaching them to observe all things as I have commanded you......." Mark 16:15-f*

TROY, ROGERS, HOLLAND

D r. Pat Henry, the State Secretary (at that time) Called me and asked me to move to Temple, Texas and attend a pastoral unity of three churches, Troy, Rogers and Holland. I would begin on Sunday morning at Rogers, the largest of the three, at 9:30 a.m. The Church service would start at 11 o'clock at Holland and the evening service would be at the Troy church. There was no parsonage at any of the small churches. I would need to rent a house in Temple. One of the dear ladies of the First Christian Church Temple, had a humongous old house where she once lived and reared her family. The unusually large house had been lifted off of its foundation by a storm and set down slightly off the foundation. Needless to say, it was a bit unleveled. We had to park our bed on the low side of the bedroom. It was not a convenient arrangement. In order to make up the bed it was necessary to push the bed slightly up the grade and prop it, so that it wouldn't roll back against the wall. Poor Marie; she was fit to be tied.

Troy was the least of the three churches, it had about 25 members. The old wood frame building sat on a small lot about 20 yards off the busy highway to Waco. In the summer when it was hot weather it was necessary to open all of the windows. The noise from the highway was terribly disruptive. There was no such thing as air conditioning for such as a small church building back in the fifties. There was a large fan. The fine people of the church were complimentary of my larger than life voice. For the first time, they observed, they could hear the preacher.

Rogers was my favorite of all the three churches. It had, possibly, two hundred members. It was a fairly wealthy farming community made up mostly of young families. There was much possible growth potential. I have several personal memories of the Rogers Church that makes it special to me. I received my first three degrees in the Masonic Lodge while serving there. The ladies of the church gave me a beautiful, gold, thin-line, engraved, Lord Elgin, pocket Watch. One lovely lady of the church was the mother of the CEO of Braniff Air Lines. She died and I conducted her service. Her CEO son gave me a round trip ticket to New York, plus a hundred dollars for expenses. That made it possible for me to attend a United Nations Seminar which never could have happened on my own time and pay. Holland was a very nice, well attended congregation. It was made up mostly of older, widowed ladies. The Church Building consisted of only a small single room sanctuary with folding chairs instead of the usual pews. The chancel area was decked with the usual accoutrements for

Christian Worship. The ladies had installed new maroon carpeting. It was a beautiful little worship center - that is, until after the following baptism was over. One of the ladies was widely over weight. I refer, especially to fat ladies, "as being fluffy." The word "fat" seems to be demoralizing to women. Any way you might take it, this lady was almost as wide as she was tall. She came up on the first Sunday I preached at her church, with the story that she wanted to be baptized and that I was the first preacher they had ever had that she considered to be big enough to baptize her. Well, not being equipped with the necessary change of clothing I offered to come back over on the following Monday evening and perform a special service of baptism.

On our way back to Temple [from Holland, Texas] we saw two boys, about 12 or 13 years old hitch-hiking. We stopped and picked them up. Minutes later on the car radio we heard the announcement that two boys had escaped from the nearby correctional prison. Through the rear vision mirror I saw them look at each other, questioningly. Without hesitating I announced to them that Temple was as far as we were going but I would let them out where they could get another ride quickly. I let them out in front of the police station. We arrived at home in time to hear the latest radio announcement, "The two escapees were back in custody. Some thoughtful citizen had dropped them off in front of the police station." Wow! Guess who?

Monday evening, at the set time I arrived at the church. The place was filled to its extreme capacity. Chairs were all filled with people, standing room only. Obviously many people from other churches as well as the usual members were present. The baptistery was filled with warm water. The only thing different was that they had a large spot light trained squarely on the baptistery. <u>It was well lighted</u>. My candidate arrived with her nice white bath robe adorning her voluminous body. I was beginning to wonder if there would be room enough in that small baptistery for the two of us. (I am not using her name for obvious reasons) After singing a song or two I read some appropriate scripture about the Baptizing of the Ethiopian Eunuch. (Acts 8:26-40) From that text, I provided a brief devotional befitting the occasion.

I was the first to enter the water and held out my hand to assist her in climbing down the narrow steps into the water. I immediately discovered that she and I together were displacing over half of the volume of water in the small baptistery. The water was spilling over into the chancel with rivulets of water rushing all the way down the nave to the front doors. People were raising their feet upon their tip-toes trying to keep their sox dry. My rule of pure pride moved on smoothly in spite of the flood. I raised my hand high, just like the artist conception of John the Baptizer. I very reverently proclaimed the words of intent. With both hands, I began to lower her fluffy body into the waters of baptism. I quickly discovered that fluff floats. When I would push the top end down the bottom end would pop up. It became necessary, if the whole body was to be covered with water to throw my left leg across her rump to hold it down. I succeeded after a couple of efforts to complete the job but it blew my holiness when the sanctuary erupted in applause.

CALL TO QUANAH

We ministered to the Temple circuit of churches for over a year, when another opening called us away. The Quanah, Texas Church was having some problems that needed a level head that would operate on a meager income. I was still cutting my pastoral *wisdom teeth,* so Brother Pat Henry called on me for that one.

First Christian Church in Quanah (Courtesy of Mary Melear)

I needed much more seminary studies, so Quanah seemed to be a gift from God with my name on it. Passenger trains, in the early fifties were still the choice mode of transportation. The Fort Worth - Denver passenger train schedule fit my need almost perfectly. I could catch the early morning train on Tuesday, arrive at TCU for the 10 o'clock Glenn Route class in New Testament. I could then study for and take classes at 1 and 3 and have plenty of time to catch the 6 o'clock back to Quanah. The long lumbering trip back was about four hours; that would give me some very valuable study time, but for one thing; the brakeman on that train was the nephew of one of the ladies at First Christian, Wichita Falls. He recognized me and knew what I was doing. That came to be one of the most faithful people I ever ministered to. The only studying I got done was when he was out doing his brakeman thing, which was a total of fifteen minutes for the whole trip.

Vernon was one of the stops the passenger train made, both going and coming back. Rev. Kenneth Teagarden was pastor of the Vernon Christian Church at that time. The Vernon church had just completed the sanctuary part of their new building. During the two years in Quanah I passed through Vernon many times both on the train and by automobile. I fell in love with the place. "Lord would it be possible for you to call me to that church?" I do not remember how many time I recited that short prayer. I seemed to hear my answer, "You are many years short on pastoral experience for that great church." Anyway Quanah was my responsibility at the time.

It seems the pastor before me had gotten all huffed up at one of the wealthier members and proceeded to "Church Him." Corbit Howard was not only Mr. Quanah he was a considerable heavy duty contributor to Texas Christian University. It was absolutely necessary that Corbit Howard get re-instated back into the church. Well, it seemed that Mr. Howard was not willing to come back to the church. He was still out of sorts with some of the other members who had sided with the previous minister. It would not be an easy task, but I felt that I was on the side of right. After much visiting with and praying for the feuding members I finally concluded that a complete rededication of every member, including Mr. Howard and his wife was the key. I spent most of Saturday night in prayer. Sunday morning came sooner than usual. "Lord this can't happen unless it is your will." The first answer to my prayer was finalized when I noted the Howard family was all present.

I don't recall what my sermon was about that morning but I do remember pointing out a fact that all of us had dared to take Holy Communion at a cost of profaning the body and blood of Christ. I then called for a rededication and things happened so fast I am not sure exactly what the activity included. I know I have never seen more hugging, sobbing and forgiving in all the rest of my days of ministry. That church came back solid and is still a great church.

I was reminded a few Sundays ago by my good friend, Mike Spiller, who grew up in Quanah, about an unusual happening in downtown Quanah back in the early fifties, during my ministerial tenure there. This big, tall Texan by the name of Jim Putman came to town. Jim had leased some wheat pasture across the road from his Medicine Mound ranch, in hopes of expanding his profits, so he had his big dappled gray gelding he called "Old Buck" in this old double long cattle trailer behind this over-size Chevrolet pickup all saddled up and ready for cow business. He always went prepared to round up any strays that might happen to be out on the road. He pulled into Fred Haynes filling station on Main street across from the courthouse and asked Fred to "filler up and check the oil." Jim needed to run into the bank and take care of some business. He had just come from Chillicothe where he had been looking at some cattle Will Yates had for sale. There were about fifty head of bald-faced yearling feeders. They would be perfect to run in on his new leased wheat pasture. Putman had made up his mind to buy them but he didn't have enough money and would need to swing a small loan at the bank.

Corbet Howard, a man for whom I came to have a great respect, was the man Jim would have to get by if he wanted to float a note at the Farmers Bank. Mr. Howard was not just a good business man, he was a great banker and you had to be squeaky clean financially if you expected Corb to buy your lien. Well, it so happened, Big Jim wasn't squeaky clean so Corb wouldn't lean. Old Jim came storming out of the bank, madder'n a Louisiana cottonmouth, jumped into his big old flat-bed rig and took off like a bat out of Georgia. His poor old cow pony, back in the trailer, was asleep and wasn't ready for the sudden slam-bang. Jim's mad-foot and fast get-away sent his sleeping horse's big fat rump whamming against the tail gate; the old latch broke open and left Old Buck *sitting* on his back-side in the middle of Fred Haynes service station. Big Jim cooled off rather shortly when he realized what had happened to Old Buck. He eased back slowly around the block a bit chagrinned, paid for his gasoline and oil, picked up some scattered fence posts and a roll of barbed wire and put them back on his flat-bed and finally talked Old Buck into climbing back into the trailer. He happened to have plenty of bailing wire so he tied the splintered old gate back together. This time he drove away gently. I have since wondered how he explained Old Buck's bent tail-bone and rear hair loss to his wife-mate. Most rancher's wives would be _nosey_ about such things.

FREEPORT CHURCH

First Christian Church, Freeport, Texas

M ission completed; where next? Reverend Frank Maybe was leaving the Christian Church in Free Port, Texas, would I go there? Sure enough the call came and I spent the next six years in Free Port. I experienced another of God's great miracles. For much of my life I had been troubled with throbbing headaches caused by a chronic sinus condition. Marie, our two boys and I arrived in Free

Port on a hot, humid Saturday evening in summer suffering, as usual, with my chronic sinus headache. The chairman of the church board was a man named Jim Shamihorn. Jim and his wife Melissa had prepared dinner for us. The dining place was in an open hallway. The salt air breeze was very pronounced and brisk. After honoring the occasion with the usual prayer of blessing, I felt my sinuses beginning to open. I grabbed the nice white napkin by my plate in time to save the potential embarrassment that could have followed. I rushed to the nearest bath room where a large amount of drainage erupted from my head. My sinus condition was immediately cured. I have never had a throbbing sinus headache since that happened.

Jim Shamihorn was the sheriff of the Brazos Port area. He had just been called to go to Washington to become a member of the FBI. The Shamihorns were moving out as we were moving in to Free Port. I had imagined that one living in sight of the Gulf of Mexico would spend a great deal of time fishing. Wrong - I never had time to do much fishing. Doc. Jones and his wife were members of my congregation. He was the captain of the Queen of Texas, a large yacht owned by the Hughes Tool Company. I went out with Doc several times. Once, Doc let me pilot the great boat all the way out from its mooring, across the inner coastal canal, out through the jetties and into the Gulf.

I had fun casting for king mackerel. Doc taught me that when people fishing from the rear deck got a strike, if I would cast out to the right side of the boat I would get a strike from the much larger male. It would be the female that struck first, with the male following her up and he would always circle to the right. The first time I did that the strike was so vicious it shattered the wood lure to bits. After that I caught a number of mackerel. Once I caught a large grouper. I made several trips with Doc and my next door neighbor who piloted a small party boat.

Once I was called by my neighbor and invited to go out with him. He had a small party of, perhaps six men from a glass factory over in Houston. It happened to be during a time when I was free so I accepted his invitation. The small party loaded a large load of beer; as I remember they loaded six cases for six men. We hadn't quite gotten out of sight of land when all six of them were hanging over the rails - sick -sick -sick. We sailed on out to the forty mile snapper banks but fishing was not one of the activities of choice. Things began to really grow hectic when a strong north-west wind blew in. And if five foot waves weren't exciting enough it became real thrilling when the tiller chain came off of the rudder sprocket. A little 20 foot boat minus the tiller, as you might guess, immediately dropped into a wave trough and sick grew sicker. Excitement? One short burst of seconds, only the sky was visible through the side ports, next only *Davy Jones locker* was visible. Finally, two of the men grew well enough to dump the rest of their beer overboard. Thank the lord for radios. The little craft was taking on a batch of water with every roll. The deck hand was too fat to make his way through the hatch door into the bilge, so there would not be any tiller chain reinstallation.

When I had seen all of the drinks stashed aboard by the party men, I cornered my pilot friend and his deck hand and gave orders that my pastoral profession was not to be announced. It was my day off. I had no intension of spending my day counseling drunks. Woefully, one of the men recognized me as the preacher who did a funeral service for some relative. My cover blew. Once again I was to be reminded just how religious a few bottles of beer can cause the unrighteous blues to loosen the tongue and flow.

Old sailors have a trick for every crisis. Our captain called one of the larger party boats that was out at the snapper banks and they came alongside and lashed our smaller boat to the side of the larger boat and we arrived safely back in port. Everybody was sober by this time and ready to listen to a short prayer of thanks for our deliverance.

I never did feel completely comfortable among those sea-faring people. After the few years there I still found myself dreaming of the dry hills of north Texas and especially the towns surrounding Wichita Falls. That would be home to me. The last days of our presence here on the Gulf we were beginning to try desperately to settle in for keeps. I had come to know and love a wonderful group of the Brazos Port families. I accepted the job as president of the Salvation Army.

As president of the SA, I was destined to learn just how sinful sin can be. One of the first things I did as president of the Army was to get the owner of one of the empty buildings in the downtown area to permit us to use the old empty store building for a headquarters. It was sufficiently large enough to put in a used clothing store and food pantry as well as office and telephone facility. I asked each of the ministers of the local churches to announce our needs at their churches. It is amazing what the fine Christian people of Free Port came up with. Hundreds of people cleaned out their closets and kitchens. It was an instant success. We had to call for volunteers to help categorize and store everything. Seeing what we had done, the local news media became interested and gave us some great advertising.

I was not surprised when hundreds of people made a run on our new store. I was surprised when I discovered that it would become necessary to make some records to keep our business honest. That worked really well for us. We did a lot of good with that service. But we began to notice that, especially one lady came back every day to get a supply of clothing of different sizes. I made some inquiries about her and learned that she never married but had thirteen children and was expecting her fourteenth. It was time for the president to go visit, I'll call her Miss Smith. I was invited in by one of her older children and ushered back to a bedroom. There in bed with a strange man was Miss Smith. That blew my mind! "What is this about?" Her answer may have been plausible to her but it rearranged all of my considerations—"O he's a nice man; he makes my new car payments for me." I passed the door of another bedroom on my way out and discovered another shocker. One corner of the room was stacked with dirty clothes almost to the ceiling. Many of the pieces I recognized as coming from our clothing store. The sheriff should be notified but what could he do? Put her in jail? Thirteen black kids? Brazoria county didn't have the money or any facility to take care of thirteen kids. How on earth was she able to take care of them? The answer to that one was a greater shock. She was drawing child support from eight different men. A visit to one of her providers was also unsettling to me. I learned that she was working *the night shift*. Sailors from the great ocean going ships always had plenty of money for such pleasure. Miss Smith would often make as much as $100 a night, when one of those big tankers pulled into port, according to my informer. He also informed me that if he missed a child support payment she was on his "a" big time. I left Free Port without knowing whatever became of Miss Smith.

About six months after my election to the Salvation Army presidency I was once more getting itchy feet. "Lord this place is beginning to eat my lunch." The heavy coastal climate was wearing me down. My weight had reduced to an especially low number for me. The hard work was a challenge that I dearly loved. The hours were constant, long and difficult but filled with exciting encounters with all types of people: rich, educated, poor and also ignorant, adults and children. The Dow Chemical Company was big in Free Port back the fifties. The greater middle class of families were well healed financially but the majority were fisher men working the fishing boats. Many of them uneducated and desperately poor.

Burglary was one of the most daring evils in the Brazoria area. One of the stories I have to remember was of a man whose wife was sickly. They had two small boys. One of the boys was about five and the other six or seven. The father worked shrimp boats. He purchased an old funeral coach and converted it into a living quarters of sorts for his family. I suppose his living arrangement was to give him more money to buy liquor and gamble. He parked his old funeral coach home down on the beach where parking was free. His little sickly wife developed pneumonia and died. There was no funeral. Her burial was paid for by the county. After his wife died he rented a small shack down near the levy, south of the Christian Church.

The shrimp boat owners all refused to employ him after his wife's strange death. Word travels fast around the fishing docks. What does Mister Coors do? (I have forgotten his real name) he turned to burglary. According to Sheriff Callahan he would make a phone call to the house he had staked out to burgle. If nobody answered he would break a window and drop one of his little boys inside to unlock the door. Callahan came to our ministers meeting and asked if we could find a place where he could place the little boys until he could find an adoption family for them. In the meanwhile he had Mr. Coors in jail.

Somehow, Coors managed to get out of jail. I suppose some of his old gambling buddies made bail for him. I was president of the ministerial alliance so he was sure that I was the one who had spirited his little boys away but for some unknown reason instead of calling me he called the Nazarene minister, Brother Harlingen, and requested that he come over to his house and pray for him. Ed. Harlingen, like any good minister took his Bible under his arm and went knocking on Coors door. Coors opened his door and very politely invited the good brother in. He then went on into his kitchen and came out with a large butcher knife and informed Ed. of his bloody intensions, if he didn't tell him where his boys were. Unfortunately, Ed didn't know where the boys were. I asked him what he did. He said "I dropped to my knees and began to pray; O Lord save this man. When I said that, he stopped and I jumped out the door and ran to my car and left there." Brother Ed said to me later that he meant to say "Lord save me from this man." But it didn't come out that way. That, no doubt, was the expression that saved him from Coors's butcher knife.

A few Sundays later, at the Sunday morning worship service while checking the faces present; as was my custom; there on the back row I saw a man and his wife that I did not know. I checked faces on the other side of the aisle and found two more strange faces. It was not unusual to see people from other churches and those with no church affiliation but these were total strangers. Who could they be? It was possible they were strangers passing through town, but not likely. Free Port is the end of the road. There was no place to go from there except the Gulf of Mexico. Two strange couples, not sitting together- hum - a pulpit committee. Where on earth could they be from?

It so happened the sermon I had planned to use that morning was not one I really delighted in preaching. It just might be a nap time job. So I gathered up my old sermon on "The Light of the World" Gospel according to John, Chapter 1.

My four faces remained behind the exiting congregation after the closing a-men. Finally I was to meet the pulpit committee, Bryan and Earnestine Stanley, Lester and Mary Gladys Blair. They would like to take Marie, our two boys and me out to lunch. They were from Central Christian Church, Vernon. Wow! "Lord why did it take so long? I prayed about that church six years ago." I would give thirty days notice to the board of First Christian Church Free Port after my resignation. That thirty days would seem to be the longest month in history.

VERNON CHURCH AT LAST

Central Christian Church, Vernon, Texas

The Church in Vernon sent a local moving van to gather us up and take us back to North Texas. The two young men that moved us were not acquainted with the heavy, Sea level Climate. They were scheduled to pack us and load us in one day. The of Free Port movers would have required three days to do the same job. It was a hot humid day. Before they had finished loading all of our belongings their clothes were dripping wet with perspiration. The humid climate was the reason for our moving back to my native land.

Our first Sunday in Vernon was a delightful time for Marie and me. The ladies of the church had prepared a wonderful dinner following the morning service. I was almost giddy with delight. One of the ladies waiting table came to take my drink orders. I ordered iced tea. When she asked would I like regular or decaffeinated my dumb answer was - "Bring me pure tea-tea." The lady (June Sanderson) held her breath until she arrived back in the kitchen. The women in kitchen all erupted in laughter. Was my face red!

I was destined to spent 10 of the happiest and most fruitful years of my ministry in that great church. Both of our boys graduated from high school while we were there. It was there that some of the business men wisely advised me to purchase some real-estate. I had lived in parsonages in all of the churches I was privileged to serve except two. When I served the Troy, Rogers and Holland churches I rented a house in Temple. My first charge, the Moran church, I commuted back and forth from Fort Worth and TCU.

ARLINGTON HEIGHTS

Arlington Heights Christian Church, Fort Worth, Texas (Courtesy of Arlington Heights Christian Church)

One Sunday, following the Easter Services in the Spring of 1970, I was standing in the Vernon church pulpit doing my usual welcoming chat while observing the familiar faces of members present and discovered another pulpit committee. Those committees are instructed to never sit together and try their best not to be obvious, but I was aware of that and saw three couples, one of which I had met a Sunday or so earlier. Mr. and Mrs. E. H. Oliver from Fort Worth were visiting relatives in Vernon as they had earlier. But who were the other two? I recalled a conversation I had with the Oliver's on another visit. Mrs. Oliver inquired of me if I might be willing to move to the Arlington Heights Christian Church in Fort Worth. I assured her that I would consider such a call, not realizing that she could be serious about my moving to a large city church especially near Brite Divinity School, TCU, Fort Worth. I never dreamed such a call would ever come for me. One of my professors had assured me, much earlier that I would do just fine in some small village church. A move to the Arlington Heights Church, Fort Worth was a compliment to my ability. "Lord is this for real?" It must have been. I spent 6 of the busiest years of my ministry there. My service there was one of the longest ministries that congregation had had since their beginning. I took a disability retirement from Arlington Heights in 1976. I was playing on a dirt bike and broke my knee. That took me out of circulation for a year or so.

It was a sad day for us when we moved out of Fort Worth. It was, indeed fortunate for us that I had purchased the Park Springs property. We had a place to call home. Being a country boy with a lot of country left in me, I was very contented, at least until the Holy

279

Spirit knocked on my door and lined me out with doing interim ministries. That turned out to last for the rest of my many years in Christian Service.

The old church parsonage of the Heights Church was no palace. It had been much abused and poorly maintained. Undoubtedly, it was the most uncomfortable of any place we had ever lived. Being about a block from the Arlington Heights foot-bridge across I 20, it was the escape route for burglars, robbers and even a murderer or two escaping back into Como. Spot-lights on the police helicopters would often light up our backyard and a loud speaker yelling, "Keep your doors locked." Such is not conducive to good sleeping.

PARK SPRINGS RANCH

Back in the early 1960s, while I was ministering the Vernon Church I took seriously some good advice I was receiving from some of the business men in the Church to invest in real estate. The Herring National Bank in Vernon financed my first purchase. It consisted of an 80-acre track with a very green valley partly shaded by a huge spreading Oak Tree. The low price, even by the dollar inflation back in the 60s I found attractive, although much of it was clay and sand stone. There was some wooded acreage that was the stopping place for the acres of topsoil blown from the fields by the south wind. The price for the 80 acres was only $75 an acre, a total of $6,000 plus tax which, seemed to me, was a bargain. There was an old house that was beyond repair. It had to be taken down.

While I was tearing the old house down, Bill Smiley, who owned the 260 acres adjoining me on the east, came over and offered me a deal to purchase his land which had a very livable bunkhouse, one that I could remember from many years ago. The old bunkhouse was once the Powers family home. My cousin, Homer Harper married Mabel, the Powers daughter. The old house was built back around 1918. Bill Smiley had removed some partition walls, built a rock fireplace and created a bath with shower and indoor kitchen plumbing. It was junky in appearance but spacious and livable. The house was furnished, even had beds, linens and towels—260 acres of good ranch land with house, all for $125 an acre. He would assume my note on the 80 acres and I would pay only six percent interest and pay once a year with as much payment as I could afford above the interest. Wow! What a deal!

RANCH LIFE AT PARK SPRINGS

All of a sudden I became a big rancher. I was offered some good advice by my banker. I should build a good fence around it and stock it with cattle. The cattle I did buy but the good fence....O well, I could prop up the old fence and it would do just fine, so I thought. My neighbor to the north was a man known as P. C. Younger. Mr. Younger proved not to be a nice man. The owners of the 80-acre track that I had purchased lived a long way off so Mr. P. C. took the fence down so he could have free grazing for his cattle. My propping up the fence was not a welcome behavior. Every time I would show up at the ranch P. C's cows would be helping themselves to my grass. I would chase them back and repair the fence. This happened over and over so I finally decided to take my banker's advice and build a good five-wire fence between me and Mr. Younger.

It worked, or did it? I arrived back at the ranch one day and found one of my cows that was supposed to have a baby calf walking up and down the north fence bellowing for her new but absent, baby calf. Well, I went baby calf hunting over at the Younger place. I found P. C. out in his cow lot trying to force one of his old milk cows to allow a strange, red and white baby calf to nurse. My greeting to P. C. was brief followed by my claim on the strange calf. My conversation quickly zeroed in: "One of my cows is missing her calf and that looks like my calf." P. C. looked over at me, squared his jaw bones up, pushed up his sleeves and replied gruffly, " Well, that ain't it." I thanked him and went back to my place. Recalling my memories of many years ago I was told of the Park Springs Bank being robbed by the Younger Brothers I decided, that wasn't my calf.

My bunk house had one smelly problem. The old wooden pylons originally used for the foundation had decayed. The floor was uneven and lay mostly on the ground. The flimsy mess had created a haven for skunks. My problem was not only the smell but late evening when we were trying to sleep the little critters were most active. I never figured out what all of their rumpus was about— whether feeding their babies, making babies or just squealing and grunting as their way of communicating.

I concluded that having skunks under your house was the worst thing that could happen. Well...perhaps not really! Finding and fixing all of the openings where they were getting under the floor was not a rewarding job because they always seemed ready to create new openings in other places. Finally, one day I went to work with determined efforts. Every conceivable possibility for their entry was solidly sealed. No way could the little critters get under my bunk-house. I had spent the day and was exhausted so it was time for me to lie back and gloat over my success. However, there was a smug little inner voice that kept telling me that something was not exactly right. Sleep came upon me but not all the way. It finally dawned on me with a start. All of those little skunks under the floor,—how are they going to get out? My *how to fix it* cells began to come together. Why not make a small opening for them to escape? I did and had another bright idea showed up. I knew about what time they went out scavenging and knew that just before daylight they would return. The way I became aware of this was that I was awakened one morning (it was snowing) just at the crack of dawn and heard this chattering sound outside my window. I looked down to the snow, saw two skunks making their way back to their favorite den, under my house. I then heard them doing what ever it was they did to settle down for the day.

Another, not so bright, idea began to take on a warm glow of pure satisfaction. What if I got up a while before they returned to my created escape hole, aimed a spotlight on the hole so that I could sit in my car and wait. Oh yea - when they returned I would unload a couple loads of buckshot in their behinds and blow them to kingdom-come. Well—they did and I did—but guess what's worse than having a pair of skunks under your bunkhouse? It's having a two dead skunks under your bunkhouse.

Like the lady who left the door to her storm cellar open and a friendly skunk found it to be a cool place to take a snooze on a hot afternoon. The lady discovered the unfriendly presence and not knowing how to deal with her smelly problem called the animal control folks for some advice. The plan was to cut up apples, sow the slices—throw some down in the cellar, up the steps and away to the woods. The ransom was to be the skunks love for apples and they would follow the pieces up the steps and away and when the skunk was away from the cellar door the lady could run between the skunk and the cellar and shut the door. That plan also worked in reverse. Her next call to animal control was that, now she had two skunks in her cellar. So, what do you do with a bunkhouse when the smell of dead skunks can't be extricated without destroying the patina on your ancient treasure? You sell it to an airline pilot whose olfactory has gone bonkers and he can't smell a thing.

While looking at some old photographs last evening of my late Park Springs ranch property I conjured up some wild memories. I was remembering the site in Park Springs where the old cotton gin once stood. The gin stood on the west bank of the huge spring for which Park Springs was named. On the other side of the spring was the Katy railroad track. The old steam trains once filled their water tanks there. There were some very large old oak trees that had been there as far back as I could remember.

The place where the spring was located was a property I very much wanted to own. I was willing to pay a good price for it but I couldn't find anybody who knew who owned it. I had dreamed of building my retirement home there. It was surely one of the most favorable home-sites I had ever seen. A man by the name of Jim Croaker did buy it and did build a good rock house on it. Jim was a retired Air Force Staff Sergeant and airplane mechanic. He proved himself to be one of my choice neighbors. He was employed by one of the rock-crushers plant in Bridgeport, Texas as a dynamite specialist. His wife, Dorothy was an RN at the hospital in Bridgeport.

The Croaker house was always wide open. There were no screens on windows or doors. Dogs, Cats, chickens, even pigs were welcome; as were the neighbors. The clear, shady, moist atmosphere was most pleasant. Air conditioning was unnecessary. It was the perfect spot. Jim and Dorothy invited Marie and me over one evening for a game of forty-two. Here begins a most exciting evening.

Marie and I arrived at the appointed time. We got all the *howdies* and *huggings* over and were shown the big, over-stuffed couch for our comfort. I noticed when we sat down there were some sounds of anguish going on under the springs of the couch. Shrill little squeaks that had to be either Mickey or Minnie Mouse being squished under our weight. Thankfully, Marie was so engrossed in conversation she was not hearing what I was hearing. The shrieking faded to a hush and things settled into a zone of quite calm. But then, did I see some teeny-weenie, little critters moving slowly along the baseboard or was it only my imagination? It was for real. As it turned out, Mickey's little family of baby mice. about one inch long, but barely had their eyes open had been displaced and were seeking a new location. All six or eight of them were inching along the wall trying to escape the scene. All went well until Bowser the Snoozer got wind of the Mickey Mouse parade. He was one excited little pooch. Jim and Dorothy had spied the little critters by then but Marie was still overflowing with conversation. A shock of attention however brought her up short. She looked and there beheld a frightening scenario fading into a live reality. She ascended on high and landed in my lap. The party ended without sampling Dorothy's delicious green Jell-O refreshments. I laughed all the way home. Marie was not so amused.

The next morning Jim came over to our place, as previously planned, to help me hook up my new electric well pump; he was also an electrician. He was still embarrassed and somewhat perplexed over our mousey evening but also a great sport about it all. Jim and Dorothy are both deceased now. They will always hold a special place in my memory.

INTERIM MINISTERIES

Central Christian Church, Nocona, Texas

I was, about that time, doing the interim services over at the Nocona Church. Jim and Dorothy joined the Nocona Church and commuted the thirty miles every Sunday just to be with us. They were a great help in restoring the old church building there. The pew Bibles, still in use there were donated by the Croakers.

Nocona turned out to be the crowning glory of the closing years of my pastoral ministering. I sold my ranch land and bought a 10 acre track of land in the edge of town. There, I built my dream house with a wood shop that became the envy of all who saw it. The old beam constructed church building was a "Carpenter Gothic" built in 1896. Some previous minister, while there had closed off the north and south transepts and made them into office and classrooms. The beautiful stained glass windows in both transepts and the east chancel window had been cordoned off and mostly hidden from view; we removed the partitions and restored the great old sanctuary back almost to its original beauty.

We constructed a fellowship hall and class rooms and offices adjoining the sanctuary as much like the early Gothic original as possible. I spent about 20 years in Nocona. I am saying it was the longest interim ministry in history. However, I did not spend all of that time with the Nocona, Christian Church. When we were called to the church, in 1977 the membership had reduced to perhaps a dozen or so members attending. The first year of our ministry there we were recorded as the fastest growing church in the whole Disciples of Christ brotherhood in the nation. Gee, it was fun!

However, during my time in Nocona, I was instrumental in enlisting two men into Christian ministry; one for the Christian Church and one for the Presbyterian Church. I also spent one year doing interim ministry for the Presbyterians Church in Nocona. Interim ministries became a rather imposing need during those years. Bowie was having trouble keeping a minister. I not only served the Christian Church there but also spent some time with the Presbyterian Church, Bowie. A host of churches followed after Bowie; Graham First Christian; Brownwood First Christian; Archer City Christian; First Christian Iowa park; Quanah First, kept me busy for a year. Then Vernon was the last one until Easter 1997.

Marie's illness became overpowering during my last days of the interim in Vernon. It was necessary to cut it shorter than I would have liked. I still glory in all of the wonderful folks I met during those years. My entire life has been richly blessed by the many churches I have served in great and small ways. After I moved to the Presbyterian Manor in 2003 I did some funerals and weddings. I Also baptized four fine young people in the Nocona Church, with the assistance of my good friend, the Reverend Jack Hill, head of the Navigators, (a world wide Christian Organization) in Wichita Falls.

In the final days of Marie's illness in Februarys of 1998 the ladies of the Christian Church, Nocona insisted that I allow them to sit with her and that I should go and attend Minister's Week at TCU. As Bob and I were driving back after that glorious time with my old class mates and professors at Brite it dawned on me just how far I had come during my many years following my collage days. I was reminded of my favorite story: *The town drunk was standing on the river bridge one beautiful moonlit night looking down into the placid waters of the river below mirroring the beauty and glory of the moon and star studded heavens. He was weeping audibly and a passer-by asked, "Old man what's the matter?" His classic reply, "Ain't nothing the matter, I yust dunno how in hell I got way up here."*

Life after Marie's passing was even more lonely than I had expected. Having spent over fifty years searching for words to bring some measure of comfort to those whose marital partners were taken in death I found most all of my efforts to have been shallow and empty. I learned that a prayerful presence can be more comforting than words. I remembered a time when she and I were faced with a most serious surgical procedure. Dr. O. L. Shelton was our pastor. He never spoke a word but he was there. His presence spoke more comfort than he could have ever spoken verbally.

I had somehow come to believe that a lengthy illness would soften the blow. Wrong, the pain of separation is always the same. Sudden death is more shocking to be sure but non the less emotionally distressing.

Some of us are more emotional than others, which only means we are swept to tears faster or slower. The period of bereavement was seemingly unending for me. I kept trying to make sense of it all. Why her and not me? What a foolish question. Would I want her to go through the emotion of grief I was left to bear? The truth soon dawned on me. I had to let her go.

I would move into a new span of life. Although I could never forget our many years together that would have to be then - this is now. I believed it necessary that I sell everything we had together and move on. She and I had always believed that Presbyterian Manor would be the place we could go together, should the time come that we were not able to live alone.

TO PRESBYTERIAN MANOR

S o, I turned my real-estate over to an agent friend, Tom Horn, and called my old church buddy, the auctioneer, Ed Garnett in Vernon who brought his large moving equipment over and loaded all of our household furnishings and took them away. Our boys picked out their desired items and hauled them away. I turned my woodworking shop tools over to Bob, my son and my grandsons and headed for Presbyterian Manor. From that point on it would be only me, *so I thought*, but no; I had this inner feeling that Marie was still with me in Spirit. Every decision I make seemed to be in accord with our will together. I ordered a new cell phone. The phone number I was assigned ended in "38", *the year she and I were married*. The Presbyterian Manor had two vacant efficiency apartments one on the second floor and the other on the third floor; Both numbers ended in "38". It was so obvious: how could I take a wrong step with such clear directions? Our two boys, Bob, John and our much loved daughter-in-law, Pat, set up my apartment in a most convenient way. Everything seemed so right.

I was much blessed as I began to meet and make many new friends, several of whom I had already known for years. I took particular notice of one dainty little lady doing her walking exercise every morning. She gave the appearance of being an outdoors, athletic type, but during her walk there would always be those headphones over her ears that seemed to be providing her with some kind of "go-go spirit" like maybe rock music. She was walking at a rapid rate as if there was some place she had to be in a hurry. It seemed she was always so focused. Actually she was listening to taped sermons; I was to learn later that she also taught Bible classes. It was not easy to get her attention. I would call out to her, "Keeping that school girl figure aren't you?" She would only turn and smile and walk on by. I learned that her name was Joan Kelley and I could not understand why I was attracted to her.

I had moved to the Manor for one purpose, to grow old and die. My mind was made up that there was no fulfilling life beyond 90 years of age. My health was rapidly deteriorating. For some reason, a small voice, plus the urging of my son, Bob caused me to try walking out on the hike and bike trail. The trail passed in a block or so in front of the Manor. I found it to be a special place for adventure as well as exercise. The year was 2004. It was springtime. I could only hold out to walk a hundred yards at first. But, in time, I began to walk all the way to the lake and back which amounted to about two miles. One day Bob and I were walking toward the lake and a lady passed us, riding a Recumbent Bicycle. It looked so inviting, with its comfortable seat and reclining profile. I immediately said to Bob, "I've got to get me one of those."

We went to the bike shop that very morning. The young man at the shop retrieved his catalogue from someplace, opened it to the Recumbent and pointed out to me that it also came in a tricycle. With my stumbling balance, I recognized that the extra wheel would be my choice, and ordered a blue one.

The first day I took my new trick out on the bike trail I could not ride more than about a half mile. I almost had to have help to stow my tricycle in the stair well and walk up to my apartment. That experience laid me up for two or three days. It took me two or three months riding my tricycle every day before I could go as far as Lake Park where the trail ended. After those few hectic rides I began to ride 10 and more miles per day. My new tricycle adventure awoke me to the realization that my life had many more days. If only I could find someone to ride with me. I tried to persuade some of the elderly gentlemen to buy a tricycle and ride with me. I had no takers. O, Pete Estes bought one for himself and his wife but never did ride them.

One day after a most exciting ride, seeing some huge birds out on the lake, the abundance of rabbits and the beauty of the wilds along the trail I was thrilled and talkative. As my fortune would have it, my little headphone wearing, hiker, neighbor, Joan Kelley who lived in 229 was sitting across the table from me and I noticed her eager attention to my lengthy yarn about my exciting morning ride. She asked me if I could take her out to the lake and see those mammoth birds. I was concerned that my tendency to slightly embellish my views along the nature trail might turn her off; but no, lets go.

After lunch, we went out and got in my Ford Windstar and were off down Fairway drive to Lake Park. The Lord must have been paying attention to my prayer. There was a huge flight of great white pelicans forming up over the park. Wow, it could not have been better. They were only about two hundred feet high. Joan was so excited she inquired, "Do you ride all the way over here on the trail?"

I drove as near the hike and bike trail as possible so that Joan could get a better view of the trail. Her next inquiry was, could she get one of those tricycles. We headed straight for the bike shop and ordered her a red Recumbent Tricycle. Neither of us had any idea about where this would lead.

Joan was all of the things I had imagined her to be. First of all, she was a lover of the great out-of-doors and the wilder the nature, the better. The first day we rode together she peddled all the way up the steep trail to the top of the lake levy, something I could barely do at that time. The next thing I knew we were signed up to ride in the Famous, Hotter Than Hell Hundred bicycle endurance run. I was 90 years old and she was 88. We both finished the 25 mile run. Joan had the time of her life. It almost killed me.

LIFE BEYOND NINTEY

I could not believe my feelings for Joan. We both had denounced any possibility of ever getting married again to anyone. But, the first thing I knew I was proposing marriage to her. She assured me that she would pray about it. I assured her that I had already prayed about it and the answer was yes. Well, two or three weeks later Joan finally said yes and we did.

We announced our wedding to be the following September 10, 2005 First Christian Church Chappell. My oldest son, John berated me saying, "Dad, do you know what you are doing?" We were married on schedule and spent the next months moving. I moved from 238 over to her much larger apartment down the hall a short distance to 229. The next thing we knew the apartment from which I had moved and the one next door were put together into a two bathroom apartment. We needed to move back down there so we could have two bathrooms. We swore we would never move again, and that we would be carried out of that apartment feet first was our firm decision, so we thought. Suddenly we found our desires to live out on the lake overpowering so that we built our honeymoon home over in Archer County on Shoreline Drive. We would spend five years in this most beautiful place, that is until my doctor assured us that we needed to move back to the Manor. We did, but found it be extremely confining for us after our roomy home on Shoreline Drive. Our little Pomeranian pooch had much to bark at there but was not permitted to bark. She was confounded.

My friend Ed Garnett had taken on a new job as a real-estate salesman. He showed us a good sized ranch out on the Red River where Bonny could bark as much as she wanted and nobody would complain. In a nutshell: Harpo Rancho Rio is the nearest place to heaven we have found. This is now our home. Joan and I are well up in our nineties but with the help of my son, Bob, who lives with us, we are as happy as can be. We have four miniature spotted donkeys, three dogs, one saddle pony and we did have a bunch laying hens but some wild grocery shoppers, like one cougar, a bobcat or two and a couple of coyotes soon consumed our chicken business.

We are now members of the Vernon Church. Our dreams of ways to serve our Lord linger on. We have had the Vernon Church people out for Sunday Church Services. That was wonderful. Our latest dream is to host a weekly Vespers Under the Stars service with a big screen to display hymn lyrics and scripture verses. We have enclosed a park area down in the river bottom under a large canopy of grapevine-laden trees by a spring-fed brook.

We have named it Bethel. There had to be a rest room there so we purchased a new travel trailer and parked it under the grapevine canopy. There is also a large tent frame between the travel trailer and the brook, that can be covered when needed. Neat huh? We are in love with it all. There is indeed, life after 90.

As we are now on our ranch:

I'm in the bucket with Joan at the controls.

Joan and I are grooming our favorite pets, spotted, miniature donkeys

John and Pat Harper (our oldest son and daughter-in-law in the back)

After these many years of observing—being human I am sure of one thing. Divine Providence, an unseen presence that precedes all earthly beginnings, is actual and dependable. There is a purpose for every human being born. Somewhere along the early days of life the purpose for being will be revealed. Most often that moment of destiny may be missed because of some overpowering peripheral influence. The Divine direction may be lost forever. But, every personality is shaped to fill some empty void. The simple adage of round pegs in square holes is a very good analogy of so many people I have met along the way.

I once attempted to fit my square persona into a number of round delusions; always the outcome was a disaster. Some might have succeeded if I had only been properly educated for that direction. Perhaps my constant inability to satisfy my void in education was part of my providential destiny. I no longer question my "if onlys and what ifs" as I once did. I have the sense that I did indeed fall much short of my professional dreams. However I come to the close of my active years in Christian Ministry with a feeling that I did my best with what I had to offer.

It is a wonderful feeling to look back over the years and note the many lives touched for the good. Such a backward glimpse of my past leaves me with the feeling that what I have sown were good seed. It is my prayer that they will result in future planting of the words of truth and life. I trust that many lives will be opened to Christian Ministry in future years. Life in such ministry is rich and fulfilling.

EPILOGUE

How Come?

Rev. Oliver C. Harper, a lonely widower of some years felt the need to move to Presbyterian Manor Upon his arrival there he discovered that his useful days were not yet over. The need of an attitude doctor there was very pronounced.

Too many fine people had come there to begin their earthly departure. Whereby Oliver. found himself cruising along in that same outside lane. He was reminded of V. O. Stamps, the Gospel Song Writer's take, *"Life's evening sun is sinking low, a few more days and I must go"* <u>attitude</u>. Old Harpo (some close friends called Oliver Harpo) decided he was not ready to take the next exit. So he moved a couple of laps over for the longer journey.

Gone but not forgotten was not a happy slogan. Witnessing so many dearly beloved becoming the dearly forgotten, Oliver began to make a list. His firm declaration was that his remaining relatives and friends would not be graced with the opportunity of forgetting his holiness or un-holiness; which ever was the pleasure of that relative or friend. He began writing and sending out Journals every so often. Some of the journals consisted of yarns about family members and friends of the by-gone years, titled The Way We Were.

Some of the names used in his narratives were changed to protect the innocent but most were out front. Most all of the yarns were based on true happenings but a few were based on fictitious stories passed on from preceding generations. His relatives and friends were reminded occasionally that if they did not respond in some way to his journalistic endeavors they would surely be exited from his list of the "Chosen." It worked wonders.

His book consists of an accumulation of the best of these, mostly true but some factitious stories. However the main purpose is to relate the conditions of the distant past to the present—THE WAY WE WERE.

So, old *Harpo's slogan:*

Now, praise the Almighty.
I'm way past ninety
and crusing on the inside lane.

CPSIA information can be obtained at www.ICGtesting.com
Printed in the USA
238686LV00003B/2/P